Snippets From My Soul

20 Years Of Hide And Seek With My True And Radiant Self

My deepest thanks to the Lucis Publishing Company for giving me their permission to include "THE GREAT INVOCATION", from "DISCIPLESHIP IN THE NEW AGE", copyright 1944, in "SNIPPETS FROM MY SOUL".

© Copyright 2007 Michael A Christie.
All rights reserved. No part of this publication may be reproduced, stored in a retrieval system, or transmitted, in any form or by any means, electronic, mechanical, photocopying, recording, or otherwise, without the written prior permission of the author.

Note for Librarians: A cataloguing record for this book is available from Library and Archives Canada at www.collectionscanada.ca/amicus/index-e.html
ISBN 1-4251-0903-9

Offices in Canada, USA, Ireland and UK

Book sales for North America and international:
Trafford Publishing, 6E–2333 Government St.,
Victoria, BC V8T 4P4 CANADA
phone 250 383 6864 (toll-free 1 888 232 4444)
fax 250 383 6804; email to orders@trafford.com
Book sales in Europe:
Trafford Publishing (UK) Limited, 9 Park End Street, 2nd Floor
Oxford, UK OX1 1HH UNITED KINGDOM
phone +44 (0)1865 722 113 (local rate 0845 230 9601)
facsimile +44 (0)1865 722 868; info.uk@trafford.com
Order online at:
trafford.com/06-2661

10 9 8 7 6 5 4

DEDICATION

This book is dedicated to our Father/Mother Creator....to our Beloved Mother Earth....to all the Masters, Angels and Guides Who work tirelessly and Joyously to help us human Souls return to our Source, especially, ... Beloved Master Jesus, A.K.A "The Christ", Beloved Master Merlin, A.K.A. Sanat Kumara, Beloved Saint Germain, Beloved Mother Mary, Beloved Paramahansa Yogananda, Beloved Gandhi, Lovable Ralph Kramden, all six billion plus of us students and teachers on Beloved Mother Earth, NOW,....may we, one day, recognize each other, since, as Beloved Gandhi once shared: "....We are all tarred with the same brush...", and most especially, to my Beloved, Beloved Elspeth who, Lovingly and Sincerely, encouraged and assisted me through every step of this book's Creation.....and last, but, most assuredly, not least.......the Co-Creator of this opus.......my deepest Love and Gratitude to...

My True and Radiant Self!

WHAT WE ARE, IS GOD'S GIFT TO US.....
WHAT WE BECOME, IS OUR GIFT TO GOD

From a plaque given to my son by his peewee baseball coach

...many years ago

ACKNOWLEDGMENTS

A special word of thanks to my dear friend and co-Heart, Kyle, without whom it would have been nearly impossible for me to get this manuscript to the publisher.

Cover design is by Jonathan Hammel who doggedly worked with me, and my Beloved Elspeth, until he captured the vision I had for this cover. For more information, you can reach Jonathan at 970-884-9821.

CONTENTS

INTRODUCTION

If someone had said to me a few days before my 40th birthday 20 years ago, that I would be penning an introduction to a book of my writings that covered the years of my life from 40 to 60, I would have said something like: "...That sounds great, but what would I write about?.."

Shortly before my 40th birthday, my life had no real direction other than going to work, paying the bills, and all the other things that most "normal" people do during the course of their day to day lives. In my case, there were one or two other complications going on but, for the most part, I was just marking time, perhaps, subconsciously, waiting for something to happen. Well, on my 40th birthday, November 25, 1986, something ONE-derful did happen and I began to get my glutei maximi in gear....probably for the first time in my life.....and absolutely nothing has been the same since then.

I was born in Brooklyn, N.Y. on 11-25-1946, the first of what would eventually be 5 children. My father had an Italian deli where, from the age of 11, I worked on weekends. I attended 8 years of Catholic grammar school (where I really did learn correct grammar....all that diagramming) and 4 years of Jesuit high school where Latin was mandatory and, because my freshman year was so great, I got to take classical Greek for the last 3 years. After my June, 1964 graduation, my high school sweetheart and I decided to get married in September of the same year........Looking back, I think we both wanted to escape from our family environments.

Before I reached the age of 21, we had 2 beautiful daughters, with a cute son arriving in 1971 (I sound like a contestant on "WHEEL OF FORTUNE"). From 1965 to 1967, I worked for New York Telephone and from 1967 to 1973, I was a routeman in midtown Manhattan. During the 1973 to 1977 timeframe, I managed my father's upscale restaurant on Long Island, where, because of my deep unhappiness with the situation there, I acquired many self-destructive habits such as drinking, gambling, etc., etc. After a terrible argument with my father in 1977, I decided, at the age of 30, to put as much distance between us as possible, all the way to Southern California, and start a new life from square one.

After a brief stint with a fast food company, because of my N.Y. Telco experience, I managed to hire on with General Telephone of California as a central office equipment installer. On account of my "New York" work ethic, always taking the extra step to solve a problem, I was promoted to a non-supervisory management position in 1980, and things just went along sort of smoothly until the approach of my 40th birthday.

I always had an interest in the supernatural...UFO's, palmists, reincarnation and anything else that struck my fancy......my mind was forever open to new ideas. A co-worker had recently done a rough version of my astrological chart, and she was quite accurate on numerous aspects of my personality. She shared with me that she was going for a "channeling", a term I was not familiar with, even though Shirley Maclaine had just published her book "OUT ON A LIMB", and she suggested I give myself a special 40th birthday present and make an appointment with a lady named Diana. It sounded like a good idea to me and so I made the appointment for November 25, 1986....the BIG 4-0.

Diana, who appeared to be my age, seemed like a sweet and gentle Soul and she took me to her office which was in the rear of a bookstore called "THE AKASHIC RECORD" (which I later learned was the name given to the record of each Soul's history from the moment of Its creation to the present.....shades of the movie "DEFENDING YOUR LIFE"). Diana explained that she only channeled the Highest Frequencies, such as Ascended Masters, and that an entity named Merlin usually spoke through her. She asked me a few general questions about my life situation and if there was something in particular I was concerned about. I explained that I had a dark secret that absolutely no one but myself knew of and that I was experiencing a great deal of guilt because of it.

Diana sat cross legged, lotus position, on a small couch facing me, then she closed her eyes and spoke the following prayer: "....The Light of God surrounds us, The Love of God enfolds us, The Power of God protects us, The Presence of God watches over us, and wherever we are, God Is....AND SO BE IT....". She began to take slow, deep breaths and in a few moments, I noticed a change in the expression on her face.... my first impression was that she resembled a little old man. When she began speaking, it was not the same voice that offered up the prayer but one that sounded neither entirely masculine nor feminine.....the speaker introduced himself as Master Merlin.

He spoke to me of many things that afternoon; how long my Soul has been in existence, my Soul's nature, some references to previous lives....all of which sounded very interesting, sort of like Yoda from "STAR WARS", but not having any real bearing on my life as I knew it. Then, about 2/3 of the way through the message, with no fanfare or drum roll, He started discussing my dark secret as if He were talking about what I had for breakfast that morning. It felt as if someone had just slammed a sledge hammer into my chest (it was sore for 3 days).....I was stunned.....how could He know about that?....I wasn't even thinking about it at the time! That eliminated mind reading as a possible explanation. Rather than chastising me for what I was doing, Master Merlin was very Loving, encouraging me to "let go" and trust in God. He said: "...You have been crying out for help for years, but don't be so limited in your thinking to believe that your plan is better than God's Plan....God knows best...".

He went on to speak of many other topics before the session was over....I was too emotionally drained after the Revelation to comprehend anything (Thank God for cassettes!)....and then He wished me a happy birthday saying that "....You have received a few good gifts today...". When Diana "came back", I asked her about Merlin's reference to my dark secret and she said that He rarely did that but He must have felt that I needed the extra "push". Was He ever right! Had He not given me that sign, I don't think I'd be writing this introduction today. But He did get my attention and, from that day on,

I began to walk the straight (gate) and narrow (way), making the first 40 years look like a summer at Coney Island.

That evening, when I returned home from work, I shared my enthusiasm about the message I received (not mentioning Merlin's reference to my secret), with Liz, my wife of 22 years. Upon hearing what I had to say, knowing how bored and unhappy I'd been throughout our marriage, she said: "....That's it. This is the beginning of the end of our marriage....". Although it would be nearly 4 years before we were divorced, her intuition was correct.....she knew that I'd found what I was looking for.....or, at least, the path that would lead me there.

Shortly after my birthday, I began to get little ideas and I started to write them down. They were usually just a few lines long and so I called them "ditties". As I became aware of different understandings, I would record them. Over time, the ditties evolved into poems and, on 8-09-1988, the 43rd anniversary of the Nagasaki bombing, I compiled a book of 35 of my poems which I called "BABYSTEPS", in reference to Beloved Master Merlin's suggestion that I not charge out and change my life overnight but, to take baby steps as I began my transformation. The poetry talked about lessons I was learning, un-Truths I was releasing, the struggles I had in dealing with those in my life who had not yet gotten the "tap on the shoulder", thus, trying to hold me back and keep me from changing, and anything else my Soul wanted to share with my personality. I just compiled the poems, and with the help of some friends, created a cover and stapled the whole package together.

Since my birthday message, I'd had 5 more channelings with Beloved Master Merlin, He was becoming a mentor, a teacher and a friend. When I would express my deep Love for Him, He would respond; "....you must Love your Self that much...and more...". He always stressed that I connect first and foremost with my own True Self. My situation at home was becoming unbearable and shortly before I put together issue 2 of "BABYSTEPS", I moved into my own apartment on 12-01-1988, eager and ready to welcome the new year. Because I was on an extended sick leave from June through September, the summer of 1989 was the best one of my life and in the fall, I started to write a different style of poetry that was often accompanied with a short essay. I had been studying "A COURSE IN MIRACLES" for the past 2 years, and many of the essays were influenced by those teachings. On 3-26-1990, the poems and writings that I had co-created with my Soul were compiled into a book I called "THE LAMPLIGHTER". That day was very profound because, as I would later discover, it was my Soul Mate's birthday.

In April, I made the trip of my lifetime, arriving in Lhasa, Tibet on 4-22-1990, Earth Day. While in that ONE-derful land, because I had never visited a 3rd world country, with all its poverty and hardship, I was on emotional overload all the time. I felt as if my Heart were expanding….I had that same pressure in my chest that I'd experienced on my 40th birthday….but it wasn't the altitude. I kept an extensive journal during that 3 week trip and perhaps I'll transcribe it some day for posterity. When it was time to leave, I couldn't bear the thought of returning to Western "civilization", but, Destiny had a most ONE-drous surprise waiting for me in California.

Upon my return to work after the trip, I had to attend a meeting in another GTC building about a mile away. After the meeting, I went to visit a dear friend named Rhonda, who worked on the first floor. While chatting with her, I noticed an attractive blond haired lady, and I asked Rhonda if she knew her. When she looked to see whom I was referring to, she lit up like a Christmas tree and said: "….That's Ellie. You two have got to meet!….", and she called Ellie over to her desk. She introduced the 2 of us and explained to Ellie that I had just returned from Tibet, and she shared with me that Ellie was planning a trip to England to take an international business course. First Ellie, then I, responded with: "….That's nice….". So much for Love at first sight.

When I got back to my office, there was a message from Rhonda to call her ASAP. She said that Ellie and I had to get to know each other better. Since my divorce would be final in a few months, and there was no one really in my life at the time, I agreed to meet Ellie under one condition: Rhonda had copies of "BABYSTEPS" and "THE LAMPLIGHTER" and I asked her to share them with Ellie. If she still wanted to meet me after reading what I was about, she could call me at my office. Rhonda agreed and, a few days later, I received a call from Ellie who said: "...I Love your writings!....They are how I feel too....". We agreed to meet in a few days, with Rhonda as the middle-person, and, after a few bumps along the way, on May 30, 1990, Memorial Day, we met after work at a local restaurant.

While the 3 of us were together, it was a bit uncomfortable but, once Rhonda departed, Ellie and I went in for dinner and all I can say is: "....It was instant comfort!...". Two days later, a Friday, we met after work and Ellie shared with me that while she was in England, she was going to go to Scotland and attempt to find her Granny's birthplace. As she was sharing her story with me, I became very emotional and my eyes filled with tears. She asked me how spontaneous I was and if I'd like to share the adventure with her. Of course I said YES! and after the weekend, on Monday morning, I booked my flight to Heathrow airport, scheduled to arrive on July 4, 1990. Our courtship was very accelerated and, 2 weeks after meeting Ellie, I let her listen to the birthday tape of my first channeling with Beloved Master Merlin. Since she was raised a Christian, and not knowing what her feelings about channeling were, I was a bit dubious as to how she'd respond to the message but, my doubts were instantly dispelled when the tape ended and she said: "...I Love Merlin!..." THANK YOU, FATHER!

A week later, Ellie and I went for a channeling where Beloved Master Merlin confirmed what the both of us already knew in our Hearts.....Ellie was my Golden Girl and we were, indeed,....MATED! When I arrived in London 2 weeks later, Ellie met me and whisked me away on a night train to Glasgow, Scotland. During the 6 hour ride, my Beloved Elspeth and I pledged our Eternal Love for each other with God as our witness....the day was July 4, 1990...another holiday.

I wanted to share how my Beloved Elspeth and I found each other, but now I'm going to try to fast forward to the present. In September of

1990, I moved in with Ellie and on February 14, 1991, Valentine's Day, we were married in the eyes of society. Ellie took a separation package from GTC in November, 1991 and I took a package in May, 1993. On 7-11-1993, we headed up the 101 highway and eventually settled in the coastal community of Seaside, Oregon. We each worked a variety of odd jobs, with Ellie finally ending up managing a bakery, and I working as a cook in the local hospital.

Because the rain and clouds were so oppressive, we decided to fulfill a lifelong dream of Ellie's by selling all of our belongings and moving to Saint Thomas in the U.S. Virgin Islands, arriving there, with our 4 duffel bags, on May 30, 1997.....7 years to the day that we first met. While the island was beautiful and the people were very welcoming to us, it was quite difficult finding a job, and our meager "grubstake" from the sale of our possessions was dwindling faster than we anticipated. So, after less than a month in St. Thomas, I called my parents in New York, asking if we could stay a few days to regroup, and arrived at Kennedy airport on 6-21-1997, 20 years to the day that I left for California. I just wanted to get a car and keep moving, but my brother offered me a job with his business on Long Island and, since there was no one or thing waiting for us, I made a one year commitment to him. Once the year was up, we spent the summer at my brother's vacation house in Vermont, working as cashiers for 3 days and having fun the other 4, and on 8-20-1998, we headed off into the unknown again, arriving in Durango, Colorado on 8-25-1998.

We rented a furnished apartment (We still had only the 4 duffel bags), and after working a couple of odd jobs, started working as cashiers for the Durango WAL-MART on 2-2-1999, Groundhog day. We moved from apartment to apartment until something ONE-derful happened. In mid-August, 2001, while considering what move to make next, the Voice in my Heart suggested: "....Live and work where you want, but please stay in the 4 Corners area....". I didn't share that message with Ellie right away, but 2 nights later she said she heard the same thing from her Heart. Since New Mexico, Arizona or Utah didn't really appeal to us, and since we already had jobs at Wally World, we decided to look for a permanent home in the Durango, Co. area.

We found a pie shaped quarter acre in a subdivision known as Forest Lakes, in Bayfield, Co., and after much weeping and wailing because of flaky contractors, we moved into our brand new modular home on 3-27-2002, the day after Ellie's birthday. We dubbed our new home: "THE CHRISTIE LIGHTHOUSE". There were many reasons why we gave her that name; she has 7 skylights and numerous windows on all 4 sides, and certainly the Love that we generate from within fills our home with Light. Also, I felt that, as times continued to change in the world, our home would, like a lighthouse, act as a beacon of Light, radiating Peace, Love and Truth to any Soul that Might be experiencing fear and need a little guidance during the possible global upheavals that have been prophesied.

After 7 ½ years working as a cashier, I left WAL-MART on 8-21-2006 when, after a brief detour in September, the idea to compile a manuscript of my 20 years' worth of writings and create a book came to me very strongly. Since I had no job, nor any prospect of one, I felt this would be a perfect time to focus all my attention and energy on this most ONE-derful project. The title for the book: "SNIPPETS FROM MY SOUL", came to me a few years ago. The subtitle: "20 YEARS OF HIDE AND SEEK WITH MY TRUE AND RADIANT SELF" came to me last month while in the "Cosmic Phone Booth" or, what is commonly known as….the shower. My Beloved Elspeth decided to stay on as a cashier, but she strongly encouraged me to finish my book before I even considered working again. WAL-MART's profit sharing plan has given me enough money to complete this Heavenly project, and for that, I AM MOST GRATEFUL!

I always said that I wouldn't consider publishing my writings until I was living them 100%, but I feel that NOW is the time to share my Soul with a few people, even though I still stumble from time to time (How ONE-derful of Beloved Master Jesus to stumble 3 times on His way to the cross). As far as Beloved Master Merlin goes, He is as Real to me as anyone else.....His Love and Energy were always quite palpable to me.....and, even though I haven't spoken to Him through Diana in 15 years, I always sense His Presence.

As I state throughout my writings, channeling is a controversial subject, and well it should be, for there are many out there who claim to speak for this entity or that, but their personalities are quite evident. Just as most doctors and car mechanics have varying degrees of ability, the same is true of people who claim to be psychic. Discernment, or wisdom, is always required, with your own Truth Checker, or Knowingness, being the final authority. We can't see radio waves or television signals, but through their receivers, we get to experience them. I was blessed to be guided to the Purest channels who spoke for only the Highest Frequencies, and for that, also, I AM MOST GRATEFUL!

Most people have not had face to face visits with all the ONE-derful Avatars Who have come to Earth to help us remember WHO WE ARE, but, for the most part, Their teachings sound and feel True to us...that's how it is for me when it comes to Beloved Master Merlin's words. Many years ago, I watched a TV show about people's experiences with angels. At the end of the show, the narrator said: "....For those who believe in angels, no proof is required. For those who don't, none will suffice...".

In order to eliminate any ambiguity, questions or possible negative responses to my writings, I'd like to offer some assumptions. When I make a declarative statement such as: "...God wants His Children to Be Happy...", please silently insert the words "I believe" at the beginning of the sentence. As Beloved Lao-tzu said: "....One who knows doesn't tell and, one who tells, doesn't know...". I believe his meaning was that the experience of God, or in Lao -tzu's case, the Tao, will be new to each of us and therefore, there would be no point of reference in our current individual vocabularies. In my Heart, I feel that God DOES want His/Her/Its Children to Be Happy. Also, most of my references to Biblical quotes or something Beloved Lords Jesus, Krishna or Buddha might have said, are not direct quotes but rather what I felt was the essence of what They were sharing.

As far as the title of this book goes, as you'll see, the snippets started out as brief ditties and evolved into multi page essays..... I suppose I might have termed the writings "footprints" instead of "snippets". Since I am playing "hide and seek" with my True and Radiant Self, over the 20 years, (Reference my poems "WHAT IS TRUE FREEDOM?" and "WHERE ARE YOU MY BELOVED SELF?"), the footprints have gotten bigger and,....the trail is getting hotter. I always thought that if I could just remember my True Identity, then all else, Really, would not matter. The fact is...I'm having FUN playing this game with my Beloved Self...it keeps me young at Heart...I'm not ready to end it and say...Come out, come out wherever You ARE.

All my life, I've always been an "acquired taste", I never had "mass appeal", but I followed my Heart and am Creating "SNIPPETS FROM MY SOUL". If only a few are drawn to my book, that's OK......to paraphrase something Beloved Master Jesus once said: "....All are called, but few choose to respond.....". When I share with people that I'm having my 20 years' worth of writings published, they ask me if writing is my passion. My response to them is: "...No, I'm not passionate about writing, but, I am passionate regarding what I write about......our collective AWAKENING!....".

GOD BLESS US, EVERYONE!

Love, Michael A Christie
11-25-2006
My 60th birthday

"THE GREAT INVOCATION"

From the point of Light within the Mind of God
Let light stream forth into the minds of men.
Let Light descend on Earth.

From the point of Love within the Heart of God
Let love stream forth into the hearts of men.
May Christ return to Earth.

From the centre where the Will of God is known
Let purpose guide the little wills of men--
The purpose which the Masters know and serve.

From the centre which we call the race of men
Let the Plan of Love and Light work out
And may it seal the door where evil dwells.

Let Light and Love and Power restore the Plan on Earth.

The above Invocation or Prayer does not belong to any person or group, but to all Humanity. The beauty and the strength of this Invocation lies in its simplicity, and in its expression of certain central truths which all men, innately and normally, accept--the truth of the existence of a basic Intelligence to Whom we vaguely give the name of God; the truth that behind all outer seeming, the motivating power of the universe is Love; the truth that a great Individuality came to earth, called by Christians, the Christ, and embodied that love so that we could understand; the truth that both love and intelligence are effects of what is called the Will of God; and finally the self evident truth that only through humanity itself can the Divine Plan work out.

Alice A. Bailey (1880-1949)

Shortly after I stepped onto my Path, on 11-25-1986, I was guided to a book titled "DISCIPLESHIP IN THE NEW AGE" which was telepathically transmitted to Alice A. Bailey by a Master known as The Tibetan (Djwhal Khul) and published in 1944. This Invocation was in the beginning of the book and I was pleasantly surprised to run across it recently. Since the book's publication, World War II was ended with the atomic bombings of Hiroshima and Nagasaki, the Korean conflict took place, then 10 years of Viet Nam, The Gulf War in 1991 and the current situation in Iraq. I can also add all the genocides carried out by tyrants such as Pol Pot in Cambodia and Idi Amin in Uganda, but the list would be too long and I don't wish to belabor the point. Still, The Great Invocation gives me Hope because, quite simply, God's Will will be done. As Alice pointed out in her introduction, it is up to us Souls to carry out the Plan.

Love,
Michael

11-25-2006

PART I

THE DITTIES

12-02-1986

Thru

2-04-1988

MY TRUTH

IF THE STILL, SMALL VOICE FOR GOD WITHIN YOU

SUGGESTS THAT YOU DO SOMETHING,

AND YOU CHOOSE TO DO IT,

THEN BY DOING IT,

YOU TURN UP THE VOLUME OF THAT VOICE,

AND MOVE CLOSER TO BECOMING THAT VOICE

12-02-1986

THE ROSE

I ALWAYS THOUGHT WE WERE LIKE ROSES,

BEAUTIFUL, BUT DOOMED TO DECAY AND DIE,

I NOW REALIZE THAT WE ARE MORE LIKE THE ROSE BUSH,

WHICH IS THEIR INFINITE SOURCE

12-04-1986

BOVINE NOBILITY

DRIVING THROUGH HIDDEN VALLEY,

I MUSED WHILE WATCHING THE CATTLE

GRAZING PEACEFULLY AND SECURE

AS THEY LOOKED UP TO WATCH ME PASS,

I WAS REMINDED OF ANCIENT ROME'S GLADIATORS

WHO ADDRESSED THE EMPEROR BEFORE DOING BATTLE:

" WE WHO ARE ABOUT TO DIE,

SALUTE YOU "

12-05-1986

RAINBOWS

IT IS SOMETIMES VERY DIFFICULT
TO BELIEVE IN SOMETHING WE CANNOT SEE,
BECAUSE OF THIS, WE WERE TAUGHT AS CHILDREN
TO HAVE FAITH IN GOD'S EXISTENCE

AS I DROVE PAST A FIELD OF BROCCOLI
THAT WAS BEING WATERED, I SAW A RAINBOW
FORMED BY THE WATER'S MIST AND THE SUNLIGHT,
AND IT CAME TO ME THAT GOD IS LIKE THE RAINBOW

HE IS ALWAYS THERE, BUT TO BE SEEN,
THE SUNLIGHT OF OUR LOVE IS REQUIRED,
ALONG WITH THE SOOTHING SPRAY
OF OUR COMPASSION AND UNDERSTANDING

12-12-1986

LIONS AND LAMBS

WHEN SOMETHING UPSETS ME AND
I ROAR LIKE A LION,
LASHING OUT WITH MY CLAWS, TRYING TO
SHRED THE CAUSE OF MY PAIN,
I AM BEING WEAK…..

WHEN SOMETHING UPSETS ME AND
I TAKE THE TIME TO REASON
THAT MY PAIN IS CAUSED BY ME AND
MY NARROW THINKING,
I AM BEING STRONG…..

IT IS NOT STRONG
TO SEE ANYTHING AS WRONG,
NOR IS IT WEAK
TO TURN THE OTHER CHEEK

12-17-1986

CHOICES

ABOUT PAIN, WHICH IN THIS CASE IS ANGUISH,

IT HAS BEEN SAID

THAT ITS SOLE CAUSE IS

RESISTANCE TO "WHAT IS"

THE " PRAYER OF SERENITY" ASKS FOR

ACCEPTANCE OF THE THINGS WE CANNOT CHANGE,

COURAGE TO CHANGE THE ONES WE CAN,

AND THE WISDOM TO KNOW THE DIFFERENCE

RESISTANCE CAUSES FRICTION AND HEAT,

WHILE ALLOWING ALL TO FLOW CAUSES NEITHER

ACCEPT UNALTERABLE THINGS AS SUCH,

AND BEGIN TO CHANGE THAT WHICH YOU CAN:

.........YOUR self......

12-22-1986

REAL POWER

IT HAS BEEN SAID THAT

THE PEN IS MIGHTIER THAN THE SWORD,

WHILE A PERSON CAN BE SMITTEN BY THE BLADE,

NOTHING HAS BEEN DONE TO CHANGE

THEIR PERCEPTIONS, AND A LIFE HAS BEEN LOST

ALTERNATELY, IF A FEW INCISIVE WORDS

ARE USED TO OFFER AN IDEA OF

UNIVERSAL TRUTH, AND ARE READ OPEN MINDEDLY,

THE SEEDS OF WISDOM WILL HAVE BEEN

PLANTED, AND A LIFE HAS BEEN ALLOWED TO GROW

12-24-1986

IMMUTABILITY

IT WAS WIDELY BELIEVED AT ONE TIME
THAT THE EARTH WAS FLAT,
THE FACT THAT MOST PEOPLE COULDN'T CONCEIVE
OTHERWISE, DIDN'T MAKE IT LESS ROUND

THE SAME CAN BE SAID OF ANYTHING
THAT DOESN'T ENJOY POPULAR ACCEPTANCE,
THE ETERNAL SOUL AND REINCARNATION
ARE VERY EXCITING CONCEPTS

WHILE EVERYONE BELIEVES THEY HAVE A SOUL
TO BE LOST OR SAVED AFTER ONE LIFETIME,
THE TRUTH MAY VERY WELL BE THAT
WE ALL ARE CONSTANTLY EVOLVING ENTITIES

TO THINK THAT I MAY HAVE EXPERIENCED DEATH
MANY TIMES BEFORE, AND WILL DO SO AGAIN,
ELIMINATES THE FEAR OF ITS PAIN AND FINALITY,
AND ALLOWS ME TO GROW AND ENJOY
THIS LIFETIME AND, EVEN MORE, THIS MOMENT

1-05-1987

PERENNIAL PLEASURE

IT MATTERS NOT HOW MUCH PLEASURE

WE RECEIVE FROM "THINGS",

BE THEY A FINE DINNER, A LONG AWAITED VACATION

OR A PROFOUND PHYSICAL EXPERIENCE,

THE MEMORY OF THESE EVENTS

FADES GRADUALLY WITH THE PASSAGE OF TIME

ON THE OTHER HAND, SPIRITUAL EXPERIENCES

THAT ARE PRODUCTS OF THE GOD WITHIN,

SUCH AS KIND WORDS, self-LESS ACTS,

APPRECIATION FOR THE BEAUTY AROUND US

AND LOVING OTHERS UNCONDITIONALLY,

BY THE NATURE OF THEIR ORIGIN, LAST FOREVER

1-13-1987

EQUATIONS

OFTENTIMES WE GRAPPLE WITH PROBLEMS
WHICH, AT THE MOMENT, SEEM INSOLUBLE,
WE SEEK EXPEDIENT ANSWERS RATHER THAN
SATISFYING AND PERMANENT SOLUTIONS

AS WITH ANY MATHEMATICAL PROBLEM,
THE CORRECT SOLUTION ALREADY EXISTS,
WE HAVE ONLY TO TAKE THE TIME TO LOOK WITHIN,
AND ALLOW THE GOD-DRIVEN TRUTH TO
FLOW THROUGH US.....UNOBSTRUCTEDLY

1-13-1987

METTLE

I ALWAYS BELIEVED THAT TEMPTATION RESISTED
WAS A TRUE TEST OF ONE'S CHARACTER,
THE WAY WE REACT TO, AND DEAL WITH, DISAPPOINTMENT
SHOULD ALSO BE INCLUDED IN OUR SOUL'S GAUNTLET

WHEN WE GET WHAT WE WANT AND ALL GOES AS EXPECTED,
OUR SPIRIT IS NOT PUT TO THE TEST,
JUST AS OUR BODIES ARE NOT CHALLENGED WHEN WE TROD
A WORN PATH, SO TOO ARE TEMPTATION AND
DISAPPOINTMENT SPIRITUAL MOUNTAINS

1-14-1987

QUANTUM LEAP

IT HAS BEEN SAID THAT IGNORANCE IS BLISS,
AND IN CASES WHERE WE HAVE NO CONTROL
OVER THE OUTCOME OF THINGS, THIS IS PROBABLY TRUE

HOWEVER, WHEN TALKING ABOUT HUMAN RELATIONS,
OUR FRAGILE ego's REQUIRE THE TRUTH
AS TO WHY A PERSON BEHAVED IN SUCH A WAY WITH US

HONESTY AND OPENNESS ARE BEACONS
THAT SHINE THROUGH THE DARKNESS OF OUR FEARS,
AND APPEAR AS BRILLIANT SUNS TO SENSITIVE SOULS

WHEN WE ARE TEMPTED TO WITHHOLD OUR TRUE MOTIVES,
MIGHT WE TAKE THE EXTRA STEP TO VISUALIZE
HOW THAT PERSON WILL REACT UPON SUBSEQUENTLY
LEARNING THE TRUTH.....

1-15-1987

INTERCONNECTION

IT HAS SUDDENLY DAWNED ON ME

THAT THE COINCIDENCES AND PREMONITIONS

WE ALL EXPERIENCE ARE NOT SO STRANGE,

AND WE WOULD SEE A CONSISTENCY

WHICH TIES EVERYTHING TOGETHER,

IF WE CHOSE TO OPEN OUR MINDS TO OTHER IDEAS

IF WE HOLD THAT THE ONLY REALITY

IS THAT WHICH WE PERCEIVE WITH OUR FIVE SENSES,

THEN ALL THE UNEXPLAINED SIGNS THAT WE ENCOUNTER

ARE MERELY DISJOINTED PIECES OF A GIANT PUZZLE

THAT HAS NOTHING TO DO WITH OUR THREE

DIMENSIONAL "REAL" WORLD

HOWEVER, IF WE BEGIN TO ACCEPT THE POSSIBILITIES

OF MULTIDIMENSIONAL, SIMULTANEOUS EXISTENCE

AND A SPIRIT WORLD WHICH IS EVERY BIT AS REAL AS

THE PHYSICAL WORLD, WE WILL BEGIN TO SEE

THE CREATOR'S FASCINATING PUZZLE START TO COALESCE,

AND MOVE CLOSER TO BEING THE GOD-CREATED

SOULS THAT WE TRULY ARE.....

1-20-1987

MASTERY

RECENTLY I WAS INTRODUCED TO A DIFFERENT CONCEPT
CONCERNING OUR PERCEIVED PURPOSE ON THE PLANET,
IT WAS SAID THAT WE CHOSE TO INCARNATE ON EARTH
TO BECOME MASTERS OF LIMITATION IN THOUGHT,
WORD AND DEED. IF WE JUDGE OTHERS OR SEE THINGS
AS RIGHT OR WRONG, FOR EXAMPLE, THEN WE ARE
FULFILLING THAT STATED DESTINY OF LIMITATION

ANOTHER SCHOOL OF THOUGHT SUGGESTS THAT OUR TRUE
PURPOSE FOR BEING HERE IS TO REALIZE OUR DIVINITY
BY ACKNOWLEDGING THAT GOD'S SPIRIT IS WITHIN EACH OF US,
AND TO ALWAYS HEED THE CALL OF OUR HEARTS,
AND NOT THE FRIGHTENED voice IN OUR HEADS,
IN SO DOING WE WILL BE WALKING IN OUR TRUTH,
IN ALIGNMENT WITH THE CREATOR, AND IN HARMONY WITH
THE UNIVERSE.......MASTERS IN A TRUE STATE OF GRACE

1 26 1987

FLUIDITY

IN MY "CHOICES" DITTY, I SPOKE OF PAIN
BEING CAUSED BY RESISTANCE TO "WHAT IS",
I BELIEVE THAT OUR BODIES HOUSE ENERGY, THE SOUL,
THAT FLOWS TO, THROUGH AND AROUND THEM,
WITH BLOCKAGES TO THAT FLOW MANIFESTED BY PAIN.
THOSE BLOCKAGES ARE CAUSED BY DIS-EASE
WHICH, IN TURN, CAUSES DISEASE IN THE BODY,
SUCH AS HEART PROBLEMS AND CANCER

WE MUST LEARN TO CLEAR THOSE BLOCKAGES
THROUGH RELAXATION, HEEDING THE VOICE OF OUR
HEARTS, AND, MOST IMPORTANTLY, FORGIVENESS OF ALL
HURTS, REAL OR IMAGINED. EVERYTHING THAT WE
ARE MUST BE ALLOWED TO FLOW UNRESTRICTEDLY
IT IS UNNATURAL TO REPRESS ONE'S EMOTIONS
WHICH ARE THE FEELINGS AND MEMORY OF THE SOUL
WHICH IS THE GOD-LIKE ENTITY THAT WE TRULY ARE

2-05-1987

THE POWER OF LOVE

AS I CONTINUE MY QUEST TO GET CLOSER TO MY HIGHER SELF,
THE MESSAGE THAT IS REPEATED OVER AND OVER
IS THAT THE MOST POWERFUL FORCE IN THE UNIVERSE IS GOD,
AND GOD'S POWER IS MANIFESTED IN HIS LOVE FOR
ALL THAT IS. THIS BRINGS TO MIND THE MOVIE "RESURRECTION"
WHERE OUR HEROINE READS A WEATHERED PLAQUE THAT SAYS:
"GOD IS LOVE AND VERSA VISA"

I BELIEVE THAT THE CREATOR KEEPS "ALL THAT IS"
IN EXISTENCE BY IMAGINING IT TO BE SO.
TO THINK THAT MANY OF US DO NOT AND MAY NEVER HOLD
SUCH UNDERSTANDINGS, AND SO, ARE NOT AWARE
THAT GOD'S LOVE IS THEIR SOURCE OF BEINGNESS, DOES NOT
ALTER THAT FACT ONE IOTA, BUT IT DOES INCREASE
MY UNDERSTANDING OF UNCONDITIONAL LOVE AND GIVING

2-20-1987

BROTHERS

WE WERE ALWAYS TAUGHT THAT LUCIFER WAS THE FALLEN ANGEL
WHO BECAME KNOWN AS "THE PRINCE OF DARKNESS"
SCRIPTURES SAID THAT MICHAEL THE ARCHANGEL USED HIS SWORD
TO DRIVE LUCIFER OUT OF HEAVEN AND INTO ETERNAL FIRE

AS I INCREASE MY UNDERSTANDING AND LISTEN TO ALTERNATE IDEAS,
I AM DISCOVERING THAT SCRIPTURES TELL ONLY PART OF THE STORY.
MICHAEL AND LUCIFER, WHICH MEANS "BEARER OF LIGHT", ARE
BROTHERS WITH EQUALLY IMPORTANT TASKS IN SERVING THE FATHER

AS THE BRILLIANT STARS IN THE HEAVENS CANNOT BE SEEN
WITHOUT THE DARKNESS OF NIGHT,
NEITHER CAN GOD'S LOVING LIGHT IN EACH SOUL BE TRULY
APPRECIATED WITHOUT THE DARKNESS OF HUMANITY'S FOLLY

3-02-1987

JUDGMENT

I AM LEARNING THAT IN ORDER TO LOVE UNCONDITIONALLY,

ONE MUST LET GO OF FEAR AND LIVE ONLY IN THE "NOW"

THIS ALLOWS US TO FORGIVE ALL HURTS; PAST, PRESENT AND FUTURE,

AND HAVE PEACE OF MIND, WHICH EQUATES TO HEAVEN ON EARTH,

WHILE STRIVING TO LOOK UPON EVERYONE AS INNOCENT AND GOD-LIKE

OUR PERCEPTIONS OF EVERYTHING WE EXPERIENCE EXTERNALLY

DETERMINE WHETHER WE ENJOY PEACE, OR ENDURE CONFLICT

SINCE WE MUST FUNCTION IN THIS SOCIETY, IT IS NECESSARY TO

TREAD THE RIDGE BETWEEN JUDGMENT, DECLARING A BROTHER TO BE

GUILTY, AND OBSERVATION, WITH THE SKILL OF A MOUNTAIN GOAT

RATHER THAN LOOK UPON A PERSON AS BEING

OBNOXIOUS, ABRASIVE OR THREATENING,

WE MIGHT RECOGNIZE THOSE ACTIONS AS FEARFUL CALLS FOR HELP

WHICH WOULD WARRANT OUR RESPONSE OF UNCONDITIONAL LOVE,

AND THEREBY EXPERIENCE THE JOY OF SERVING THE FATHER

3-31-1987

UNIVERSAL TWINS

AS I CONTINUE THIS JOURNEY OF DISCOVERING MY HIGHER SELF,
THE MESSAGE THAT EACH LESSON HAS TWO SIDES
IS GENTLY REPEATED TO ME OVER AND OVER AGAIN

PATIENCE AND TRUST COMPRISE A SINGLE DOUBLE-EDGED SABRE
WHEN WE TRUST THE WISDOM OF THE UNIVERSE UNCONDITIONALLY,
THE INNER PEACE THAT PATIENCE PROVIDES WILL FOLLOW

ANOTHER SET OF UNIVERSAL TWINS INCLUDES TEACHER AND STUDENT
WHEN BEINGS INTERACT, A LEARNING PROCESS TAKES PLACE
THE ONE TEACHING THE LESSON IS BEING TAUGHT AT THE SAME TIME

IN ORDER TO INCREASE ONE'S AWARENESS, IT IS NECESSARY
TO TAKE THE EXTRA STEP OF LOOKING BEYOND THE IMMEDIATE
AND DISCOVERING ITS COSMIC COUNTERPART

5-07-1987

SIMPLE TRUTH

YOU WILL ALWAYS RECOGNIZE THE TRUTH

WHEN YOU ENCOUNTER IT

AND ARE WILLING TO RECEIVE ITS MESSAGE

WITH AN OPEN HEART AND UNCLOUDED PERCEPTION

THE TRUTH NEVER TRUMPETS ITS ARRIVAL,

OR THROTTLES YOU INTO SUBMISSIVE ACCEPTANCE

IT GETS YOUR ATTENTION BY GENTLY TAPPING YOU ON THE

SHOULDER, AND ALLOWING YOUR SOUL TO DO THE REST

5-18-1987

BALANCE

THROUGHOUT THE YEARS, POETS AND PHILOSOPHERS

HAVE ESPOUSED THE WISDOM OF HEEDING ONE'S HEART

RATHER THAN THE ego DRIVEN MIND

THIS IS NOT TO SAY THAT THE MIND IS USELESS

AND HAS NO PURPOSE IN OUR LIVES;

NOTHING IS WASTED IN THE UNIVERSAL PLAN

I HAVE COME TO REALIZE THAT THE MIND IS AN EXCELLENT TOOL

THAT IS TO BE USED BY A SKILLED (H)ARTISAN

THE HEART FIRST CREATES THE IDEAS IN OUR LIVES

AND THEN USES OUR MINDS AND BODIES

TO DEFTLY SHAPE OUR THOUGHTS AND ACTIONS

AND FINISHES ITS ARTWORK WITH A DOUBLE COAT OF TRUTH

7-03-1987

BALANCE II

THE TRUTH MAY SOMETIMES STING THE ego

BUT IT IS, AT THE SAME TIME, A SOOTHING BALM

WHEN IT IS RECEIVED WITH AN OPEN HEART

7-20-1987

LIVING ONE'S TRUTH

"TO THINE OWN SELF BE TRUE" HAS A DEEPER MEANING FOR ME NOW
WHAT IS TRUE FOR ONE PERSON MAY NOT BE TRUE FOR ANOTHER
NEITHER ONE IS RIGHT OR WRONG, BECAUSE I'M DISCOVERING THAT
TRUTH IS LIKE TASTE, THERE'S NO WAY YOU CAN ARGUE OVER IT

WE EACH CREATE OUR OWN WORLD WITH OUR BELIEFS, OR TRUTH
TEN DIFFERENT PEOPLE CAN LOOK AT THE SAME SITUATION
AND HAVE COMPLETELY DIFFERENT PERCEPTIONS OF IT, WITH EACH
PERHAPS THINKING THAT THE OTHER NINE ARE A BIT CONFUSED

THE IMPORTANT THING IS TO ACKNOWLEDGE THAT EVERYONE
HAS THEIR OWN TRUTH AND IS ENTITLED TO IT
IT DOESN'T MATTER WHETHER YOU AGREE WITH IT OR NOT
JUST HONOR IT AS YOU WOULD HAVE YOUR OWN TRUTH HONORED

I AM LEARNING THAT AN ACTION TAKEN IN ONE'S TRUTH
CAN NEVER BE WRONG, THOUGH IT MAY DRAW A LESSON TO GROW BY
WE CREATE OUR OWN PAIN VIA OUR MISPERCEPTION OF THE LESSON
ONE SHOULD NEVER BE IN PAIN, IF THEY ARE LIVING THEIR TRUTH

7-30-1987

SHADES

WHEN PEOPLE WOULD SAY THAT I WAS
LOOKING AT THE WORLD THROUGH "ROSE COLORED" GLASSES,
I TOOK THEIR MEANING TO BE THAT I WASN'T
FACING THE HARSH REALITIES OF LIFE
I'M LEARNING THAT THE "HARSH REALITIES" BELONGED TO THEM
AND THEY WERE MINE TOO, IF I CHOSE TO ACCEPT THEM
AS A PART OF MY TRUTH, WHICH IS MY REALITY

NOW THAT I BELIEVE THAT MY THOUGHTS AND WORDS
PHYSICALLY CREATE MY PRESENT AND FUTURE EXPERIENCES,
I REALIZE THAT LOOKING AT LIFE THROUGH TINTED GLASSES
IS SOMETHING THAT SHOULD BE ENCOURAGED
A PERSON CAN LOOK IN THE MIRROR AND SAY "I LOVE YOU" OR
"I DON'T LOVE YOU"...THE CHOSEN PHRASE WILL BEGIN TO
CREATE EITHER A DREAM EXISTENCE, OR PERPETUATE
A LIVING NIGHTMARE.....

8-12-1987

GROWTH

I HAVE RECEIVED A NEW PERSPECTIVE ON NEGATIVITY AND ITS
PURPOSE IN OUR LIVES. SINCE I BELIEVE EVERYTHING HAS LOVE
AS ITS SOURCE, NEGATIVITY IS ALSO A FORM OF LOVE, JUST WITH A
LOWER VIBRATION THAN THAT TO WHICH WE ARE ACCUSTOMED

IT IS THROUGH NEGATIVITY THAT WE ARE ABLE TO GROW,
SINCE IT AFFORDS US A CHOICE OF TWO OPPOSITES
THE CHOICE ITSELF, AND THEN HOW WE DEAL WITH IT,
DETERMINE OUR RATE OF GROWTH
AND WHETHER OR NOT WE WILL CAUSE PAIN FOR OURSELVES

IF WE ALTER OUR BELIEFS TO ENABLE US TO VIEW NEGATIVITY
AS AN OPPORTUNITY TO ADVANCE SPIRITUALLY,
THEN THERE WILL BE NO PAIN AND WE WILL WITNESS
THE MIRACLE OF CHANGED PERCEPTIONS,
WHICH WILL CREATE A NEW SET OF EVENTS IN OUR LIVES

AS THE SEED THAT IS PLANTED IN THE EARTH
MUST WORK ITS WAY THROUGH THE SOIL TO THE SUNLIGHT,
SO MUST WE FIRST WORK THROUGH OUR TRIALS AND LESSONS
IN ORDER TO GROW UNFETTERED AND UNLIMITED,
NURTURED BY THE SUNSHINE OF OUR FATHER'S LOVE
9-02-1987

ETERNITY

"HOW LONG IS FOREVER?" IS A QUESTION
THAT IS IMPOSSIBLE TO ANSWER IN OUR TERMS,
SINCE WE EXIST IN A FINITE WORLD,
WE CANNOT IMAGINE SOMETHING THAT HAS NO END,
OR EVEN LASTS A BILLION YEARS, FOR THAT MATTER

THE SEASONS COME AND GO, LEAVING BEHIND
MEMORIES OF WHAT OCCURRED DURING THEIR TIME
WE ALL ACKNOWLEDGE THE CYCLE OF BIRTH AND DEATH,
AND ALTHOUGH SOME KNOW THAT DEATH IS AN ILLUSION,
MANY FEEL LIMITED TO THE FEW YEARS OF LIFE WE ARE AWARE OF

AN IMPORTANT PART OF MY NEW BELIEFS IS
TO LIVE IN THE MOMENT, ENJOYING IT FULLY,
SINCE IT IS ALWAYS "NOW" WHEREVER WE ARE,
IF WE STAY IN THE NOW, WE ARE EXPERIENCING ETERNITY
AND THE ABSOLUTE PEACE OF MIND THE "ETERNAL NOW" BRINGS

9-11-1987

DIRECTION

I OFTEN THOUGHT OF MYSELF AS A HUMMINGBIRD,
PLEASANT TO WATCH AND LISTEN TO
BUT NEVER STAYING IN ONE PLACE TOO LONG,
AND ALWAYS KNOWING WHICH WAY IT WAS GOING

SINCE FOLLOWING MY HEART UNCONDITIONALLY,
I NOW FEEL LIKE A FEATHER IN THE WIND
THAT KNOWS NOT WHEN THE DIRECTION WILL CHANGE,
BUT HAS ABSOLUTE TRUST IN ITS GUIDING WISDOM

MANY HAVE GONE OFF TO FIGHT A WAR THAT
THEY NEITHER WANTED NOR BELIEVED IN,
LEAVING THEIR LOVED ONES BEHIND TO WONDER
IF AND WHEN THEY WOULD HAVE TO OFFER THE ULTIMATE

GOD IS NOT ASKING ME TO SACRIFICE MY ILLUSORY EXISTENCE,
BUT RATHER TO FULFILL THE CONTRACT I SIGNED
TO HELP TRANSFORM OUR PLANET INTO A SHIMMERING JEWEL
THAT MANIFESTS HIS PEACE, LOVE AND TRUTH

THE DAYS OF MARTYRDOM ARE OVER AND DONE WITH,
TO REMIND MYSELF OF THIS FACT, I MUST REMEMBER
THAT GOD NEVER TAKES SOMETHING AWAY WITHOUT REPLACING IT
WITH SOMETHING BETTER AND FAR MORE BEAUTIFUL

9-16-1987

LINKUP

EVER SINCE I STARTED MY SPIRITUAL JOURNEY,
I HAVE HEARD OVER AND OVER THAT
ONE MUST LOOK WITHIN FOR ALL THAT THEY SEEK
AT FIRST, THIS WAS VERY PUZZLING TO ME,
SINCE I COULDN'T CONCEIVE OF ANYTHING INSIDE ME
EXCEPT MY 3 DIMENSIONAL ORGANS, MUSCLES AND BONES

AS I CONTINUE TO INCREASE MY AWARENESS HOWEVER,
I UNDERSTAND THAT GOD'S SPIRIT DWELLS WITHIN MY SOUL
AND APPEARS AS A SPARK OR TINY STAR THAT ENLIVENS MY BEING
THIS SPARK OF GOD PROVIDES ME WITH THE LOVE I SEEK,
THE WISDOM AND GUIDANCE I NEED, AND THE TRUTH
THAT LIBERATES ME FROM THE GRIP OF FEAR

THEREFORE, IF ONE SEEKS OUTSIDE THEMSELVES FOR ANYTHING,
IT IS AN INDICATION THAT THE STAR IS PARTIALLY OBSCURED
AND THERE IS A DARKNESS WITHIN THAT MUST BE DISSOLVED
THIS CAN BE ACCOMPLISHED BY LINKING UP WITH ONE'S SOUL
AND PURIFYING OUR BEINGS OF ALL NEGATIVITY IN THOUGHT,
WORD AND DEED, CLEARING THE WAY FOR GOD'S RADIANT
LIGHT TO SHINE THROUGH UNOBSTRUCTED, FOR ALL TO SEE

9-24-1987

COMMITMENT

A RECENT "SILLY" STUDY ILLUSTRATED THAT
THERE WERE 250 DIFFERENT WAYS TO WASH THE DISHES
IF SUCH A SEEMINGLY SIMPLE TASK HAS SO MANY VARIATIONS,
HOW MANY APPROACHES ARE THERE TO LIVING A LIFE?

A PERSON CAN GO TO AN ISOLATED SPOT IN THE WOODS,
PUT THE BARREL OF A LOADED .38 IN THEIR MOUTH,
AND THINK THAT THEY'RE PULLING THE TRIGGER TO ETERNITY
SANE OR NO, THEY WERE COMMITTED

WHETHER ONE AGREES WITH THE ACTION OR NOT,
IT MUST BE AGREED THAT THE COMMITMENT WAS TOTAL,
TAKEN A STEP FURTHER, IT CAN BE SEEN THAT ANY REAL
COMMITMENT REQUIRES A 100% EFFORT

THE AFOREMENTIONED IS AN EXAMPLE OF A COMMITMENT TO
SUICIDE, OR AN ATTEMPT AT SIDESTEPPING A LESSON
ACCORDING TO THE LAWS OF REINCARNATION, THAT PERSON
WILL HAVE TO FACE THE SAME LESSON AGAIN IN ANOTHER LIFE

IF ONE HAS SUCH ABILITY TO ANSWER THE CALL OF THEIR ego,
HOW WOULD THAT SAME PERSON, OR ANYONE ELSE,
ANSWER GOD'S CALL TO LIVE UP TO THE CONTRACT THEY SIGNED
AND COMMIT TO THE TASK THEIR SOUL AGREED TO BEFORE BIRTH?

10-02-1987

METAMORPHOSIS

AS I CONTINUE MY EVOLVEMENT TOWARDS MY TRUE SELF,
I AM LEARNING TO PEER BEYOND "THE LOOK OF THINGS"
THIS IS NO NEW REVELATION, BUT RATHER AN ANCIENT TRUTH
THAT REMINDS ME, ONCE AGAIN, THAT ALL KNOWLEDGE
IS WITHIN ME AND JUST NEEDS TO BE "DUSTED OFF"

WE HAVE ALL HEARD THIS STATED MANY TIMES IN DIFFERENT WAYS:
"BEAUTY IS ONLY SKIN DEEP", AND
"YOU CAN'T TELL A BOOK BY ITS COVER",
ARE TWO EXAMPLES THAT ILLUSTRATE THE SAME POINT

DURING THESE TIMES OF RAPID FIRE EVERYTHING,
IT IS MUCH EASIER TO LABEL SOMEONE
AS A CERTAIN TYPE OF PERSON WHO IS EXPERIENCING "WHATEVER",
RATHER THAN TAKE THE TIME TO DISCOVER
THE RADIANT BEING BENEATH THE ego's FAÇADE

MANY CAN MARVEL AT A BEAUTIFUL MONARCH BUTTERFLY,
ENJOYING ITS SPLENDID COLORS AND GRACEFUL FLIGHT,
AND FORGET THAT IT WAS ONCE AN UNGAINLY CATERPILLAR
THAT SPUN ITS SILKY COCOON AND USED IT FOR PROTECTION
WHILE IT GREW AND CHANGED ITS FORM.....BUT NOT ITS SPIRIT!
10-22-1987

ATTACHMENT

AT TIMES WHEN I FEEL THAT MY SPIRITUAL JOURNEY
IS ON A STRAIGHT TRACK, GOING FULL SPEED,
SOMETHING HAPPENS IN MY MIND THAT CAUSES ME
TO SEEMINGLY RETURN TO SQUARE ONE
AND NEGATE ALL THE PROGRESS THAT I'VE MADE,
AS IF I WERE TETHERED TO A LARGE RUBBER BAND

THE MORE I OBSERVE THIS PHENOMENON TO UNCOVER
THE REASONS FOR REVERTING BACK TO MY OLD HABITS,
I FIND THE ROOT CAUSE STEMS FROM THAT ASPECT OF ME
THAT KNOWS ONLY FEAR IN ITS MANY UGLY FORMS
MY ego IS THE ATTACHMENT THAT KEEPS PULLING ME BACK,
AND THAT TRUTH WILL SET ME FREE

10-23-1987

FACETS

I HAVE WRITTEN EARLIER ABOUT EACH PERSON HAVING
THEIR OWN TRUTH, OR BELIEFS, AND BEING ALLOWED
TO LIVE THEM WITHOUT REPROACH FROM OTHERS
WHO HAVE AN ENTIRELY DIFFERENT BELIEF SYSTEM

THE IMPORTANT THING IS TO LIVE YOUR TRUTH,
AND BE A SHINING EXAMPLE OF IT,
ALWAYS KEEPING AN OPEN HEART AND MIND,
WHILE ALLOWING OTHERS TO DO THE SAME

IN THE END, WE WILL SEE THAT EACH PERSON'S TRUTH
IS A SMALL PART OF THE UNIVERSAL TRUTH OF GOD,
JUST AS A SINGLE FACET DOES NOT REPRESENT THE ENTIRE
JEWEL, NEITHER DO OUR OWN BELIEFS REPRESENT
ALL OF GOD'S TRUTH......

10-28-1987

FORMS

THROUGHOUT OUR LIVES, WE PLAY MANY DIFFERENT ROLES
AND ASSUME A VARIETY OF PERSONALITIES AND FORMS,
WE ARE SOMEONE'S CHILD AND GRANDCHILD, COUSIN AND CLASSMATE,
CO-WORKER, SIBLING, SPOUSE, PARENT AND FRIEND,
THE COMMON THREAD THAT RUNS THROUGH ALL THE VARIOUS FORMS
IS OUR TRUE SELF WHOM WE SEEM NEVER TO REALLY ALLOW
THE PROPER TIME TO DEVELOP AND GROW TO FULL MATURITY

I FEEL THAT CERTAIN PEOPLE REACH A POINT IN THEIR LIVES
WHEN THEY DECIDE TO BE WHO THEY TRULY ARE,
AND LOVE WHO THEY ARE, AND DO ALL THAT THEY CAN DO,
RELINQUISHING ALL THE PREVIOUS FORMS THEY PROJECTED
FOR THE ONE THAT WILL MAKE THEM HAPPIEST
AND MOST PRODUCTIVE. WHEN THEY DO THIS,
THEY WILL SEE A FORM OF DIVINE LIGHT AND LOVE THAT KNOWS
NO FEAR OR WANT AND IS CONTENT JUST TO BE

11-05-1987

JOURNEY

I RECENTLY READ A QUOTE FROM THOREAU

WHERE HE STATED THAT ONE WHO GOES ALONE

CAN BEGIN THE TRIP IMMEDIATELY,

WHILE ONE WHO TRAVELS WITH ANOTHER

MUST WAIT UNTIL THAT OTHER IS READY

WHILE I CAN MOST CERTAINLY RELATE TO HIS MESSAGE,

I FEEL THAT HE MUST HAVE BEEN REFERRING TO

ANOTHER PERSON WHEN HE SPOKE OF TRAVELLING WITH "ANOTHER"

FOR, SINCE I BEGAN THE WORK OF LINKING UP WITH MY SOUL,

I HAVE NEVER FELT MORE "UN-ALONE" IN MY LIFE

I HAVE BEGUN EXPERIENCING AN INNER PEACE

THAT HAS ELUDED ME FOR MY ENTIRE TIME ON THE PLANET

AND, WHEN I RECORD A DREAM, WHICH IS MY SOUL'S MEANS

OF MARKING MY PROGRESS AND PROVIDING GUIDANCE,

I KNOW ABSOLUTELY THAT I AM NOT ALONE ON MY JOURNEY

12-01-1987

MIRRORS

SAGES HAVE STATED THROUGHOUT HISTORY, THAT THE ONE WHO UPSETS YOU MOST IS YOUR GREATEST TEACHER, SINCE THAT WHICH ANNOYS YOU IS MERELY A REFLECTION OF SOMETHING WITHIN YOU, AND THERE IS A LESSON TO BE LEARNED. WITHIN THAT "OTHER", YOU CAN EITHER FIND OR LOSE YOUR TRUE SELF

THIS SOUNDS TRUE TO ME, AND I HAVE BEGUN TO LOOK AT MY ANGER WITH DISCERNMENT FOR, THERE ARE TIMES WHEN THINGS MUST BE SAID, AND IF THEY ARE SOMETIMES STATED IN ANGER, THAT IS ACCEPTABLE, PROVIDED THE ANGER IS NEITHER PROTRACTED NOR ACCUSATORY.......

HOWEVER, IF IN OUR ANGER, WE POINT THE FINGER AND self-RIGHTEOUSLY PROCLAIM OURSELVES TO BE ABOVE SUCH ACTIONS OR BELIEFS, WE MUST BE SCRUPULOUSLY HONEST WITH OURSELVES AND LOOK AT THE OBJECT OF OUR self-DECEIVING TIRADE, AND KNOW THAT WE ARE MERELY PEERING INTO A MIRROR

12-03-1987

DREAMERS AND TRAVELERS

ONCE A PERSON HAS BEGUN TO AWAKEN,

THEY CAN NO LONGER TRAVEL

WITH ONE WHO IS STILL ASLEEP

THEY CAN NEITHER WAIT FOR THE SLEEPER,

FOR THEN THE COSMIC TRAIN WILL BE MISSED,

ALONG WITH ALL THEY WOULD HAVE ENCOUNTERED

NOR, MAY THEY TRY TO ROUSE

THEIR COMATOSE COMPANION,

FOR EACH REQUIRES DIFFERING DEGREES OF SLEEP

SOONER OR LATER, ALL WILL AWAKEN

TO GREET THE GLORIOUS SUN,

MARKING THE BEGINNING OF A NEW DAY, AND LIFE

1-14-1988

BOOMERANG

IF, TO LOVE ANOTHER AND DO GOOD FOR ANOTHER
IS TO LOVE AND DO GOOD FOR ONE'S SELF,
BECAUSE OF THE LOVE THAT WE FEEL FOR OUR SELVES
UPON EXPRESSING OUR LOVE FOR OTHERS

THEN, IN ORDER TO HAVE BALANCE, IT MUST FOLLOW THAT
TO STRIKE OUT AT ANOTHER,
OR HAVE ANY NEGATIVE FEELINGS TOWARD ANOTHER,
WE ARE REALLY STRIKING OUT AT
AND DISLIKING OUR SELVES.....

THIS HELPS ME UNDERSTAND WHY JESUS TAUGHT US
THAT WE <u>WOULD</u> LOVE OUR NEIGHBORS
AS WE LOVED OUR SELVES, AND TO ALWAYS TURN
THE OTHER CHEEK, TO LET THE ONE STRIKING
SEE THAT THEY ARE ONLY STRIKING THEMSELVES

2-04-1988

PART II

THE "BABYSTEPS" POETRY

4-28-1987

Thru

4-06-1989

'TIS MORE FUN TO PEER BEYOND THE LOOK OF THINGS

"THE VEIL"

DRIVING THROUGH HIDDEN VALLEY
PAST A GREY AND DEWY TREE,
I THOUGHT OF THE SURROUNDING BEAUTY
THAT, FOR THE FOG, I COULD NOT SEE

HAD A STRANGER HAPPENED TO PASS BY
THIS DARK AND DREARY PLACE TODAY,
HARD PRESSED WOULD THEY BE TO REFLECT:
"WHAT A PARADISE TO GET AWAY!"

I THOUGHT OF THE VEIL OF WORLDLINESS
THAT SHROUDS OUR INNER SIGHT,
PREVENTING OUR GOD-LIKE ESSENCES
FROM GAZING UPON THE LIGHT

BEYOND THAT VEIL EXISTS FOR US
A WORLD WHERE FEAR IS UNHEARD OF,
ANOTHER WAY TO SHARE OUR LIVES
PROTECTED BY THE POWER OF LOVE

WHAT GLORY UNFOLDED BEFORE MY EYES
AS THE MORNING SUN BURNED ITS WAY THROUGH,
MOUNTAINS AND MEADOWS AND TREES TO SPARE
MANIFESTING OUR FATHER'S LOVE SO TRUE

YET, THERE'S A SECOND LESSON THAT'S CRYSTAL CLEAR:
WE ALL ARE SOULS THE WORLD CAN'T SEE,
I MUST REMEMBER THAT BENEATH THE VEIL
SHINES A BEING WITH GOD'S DIVINITY

4-28-1987

I BELIEVE THAT WHEN THIS EVENT WAS TAKING PLACE, SKEPTICS REFERRED TO IT AS THE "MORONIC CONVERGENCE"

"THE HARMONIC CONVERGENCE"

THE MORE I SEE AND CHOOSE TO BE ME,
THE MORE I UNDERSTAND
THAT MY PRESENCE UPON OUR PRECIOUS PLANET
IS PART OF THE MASTER PLAN

AS THE SUN AND THE MOON ARE IN PERFECT TUNE,
MANIFESTING GOD'S HARMONY,
SO, MY self AND MY SOUL HAVE AS THEIR GREAT GOAL
TO UNITE AND HELP THE WORLD SEE

FOR, I FEEL THAT THE EARTH HAS AS MUCH WORTH
AS EACH OF GOD'S CREATIONS,
AND IT'S ONLY THE FEAR OF "NOT ENOUGH HERE"
THAT SEPARATES THE NATIONS

THIS HISTORIC TIME, SEEN BY THE MAYANS,
LONG BEFORE OUR MOST RECENT BIRTH,
MARKS THE BEGINNING OF THE END OF FEAR AND DREAR
AND THE START OF HEAVEN ON EARTH

SO, AWAKEN BROTHERS AND SISTERS ALL
AND HEED THE UNIVERSE'S CALL,
TO ROUSE YOURSELVES FROM YOUR SLEEPY BERTH,
AND BECOME A CARETAKER OF PLANET EARTH

8-16/17-1987

"...DIO VEDE E PROVIDE...", GOD SEES AND PROVIDES, ONE OF MY BELOVED POPPA'S FAVORITE PHILOSOPHIES

"SUBSTANTIAL FLOW"

AS THE BIRDS IN THE TREES AND THE FISH IN THE SEAS
HAVE ALL THEIR REQUIREMENTS MET,
TOO, THE GEESE IN THE POND AND THE DOE WITH HER FAWN
ENJOY MEALS THAT ARE HEAVEN SENT

THIS TRUTH WARRANTS A NEED TO LOOK AT MAN'S GREED
AND RELUCTANCE TO SHARE AND SHARE,
HE'D RATHER COVET AND HOARD, AND EVEN WAGE WAR,
FOR FEAR THAT "THERE'S NOT ENOUGH THERE"

THE ROOT OF ALL FEARS CAN BE TRACED THROUGH THE YEARS,
TO PERCEPTIONS BASED ON ILLUSION,
CITING SHORTAGE AND PAIN, IF THERE'S NOT ENOUGH GRAIN
OR WATER TO DRINK AND BATHE IN

THE TRUTH, AS SOME KNOW, CLAIMS A BOUNTEOUS FLOW
OF ALL THAT GOD CREATED,
AND IT'S ONLY THE DAMS CONSTRUCTED BY MAN
THAT PREVENT ALL FROM BEING SATED

FOR HOW CAN A MAN NEED MORE THAN HE NEEDS
TO LEAD A HAPPY LIFE,
UNLESS, THE WORD NEED, REALLY MEANS GREED,
EQUATING TO SORROW AND STRIFE

8-20-1987

THE ANCIENT GREEKS ADVISED: "KNOW THY SELF"... BELOVED MASTER JESUS ADVISED: "SEEK FIRST THE KINGDOM OF HEAVEN WITHIN YOU"...IN "10", MIKEY ADVISED: "SEEK NOT OUTSIDE YOUR SELF FOR ANYTHING"

"RELATIONSHIPS"

IN MANY OF THE SONGS WE HEAR TODAY,
THE THEME IS ALWAYS A PLAINTIVE "PLEASE STAY",
THE IMPLICATION BEING THAT ONE IS NOT WHOLE
UNLESS THEY ARE JOINED WITH ANOTHER SOUL

THIS TYPE OF THINKING HAS GONE ON FOR YEARS,
PREYING UPON OUR PRIMAL FEARS
OF BEING ALONE , PLAYING SOLITAIRE
BECAUSE THERE'S NO ONE ELSE TO CARE

AND SO WE SEARCH AND COMPROMISE,
DECEIVING OURSELVES WITH LITTLE "WHITE LIES",
CLAIMING THAT HAPPINESS IS ALL ABOUT,
NEVER WITHIN, ALWAYS WITHOUT

A "NEW" PHILOSOPHY IS IN ITS YOUTH,
BASED UPON GOD's PEACE, LOVE AND TRUTH,
TEACHING US THAT BECOMING COMPLETE
IS AS EASY AND PAINLESS AS CROSSING THE STREET

THE REQUIREMENT IS SIMPLY A STRONG DESIRE
TO IDENTIFY WITH THE SPARK OF GOD'S GLORIOUS FIRE,
ALL THAT ONE NEEDS TO BE TRUE AND WHOLE
IS TO ALLOW THE SAGE GUIDANCE OF THEIR INFINITE SOUL

PEOPLE WHO CLAIM THIS TRUTH TO KNOW,
PERMIT EACH OTHER TO LEARN AND GROW,
AND, RATHER THAN SEEK TO BLOCK AND IMPAIR,
WISELY OFFER THEIR LIVES TO SHARE

10-10-1987

A WISE MASTER ONCE DESCRIBED "PATIENCE" AS:
"...THE DISTANCE, IN TIME, BETWEEN AN IDEA AND ITS MANIFESTATION..."

"THE PEACE OF PATIENCE"

THERE'S A QUESTION I OFTEN POSE TO ME,
TO HELP ME VIEW WHAT I MIGHT BE
IF THE GRUELING GRIND OF TOIL AND STRIFE,
WERE NO LONGER A PART OF MY DAILY LIFE

IT'S NOT THAT WORK REPULSES ME,
OR THE PEOPLE I MEET DON'T HELP ME SEE,
IT'S SIMPLY THAT THE GAME IS OLD,
AND I FEEL IT'S TIME FOR SOMETHING BOLD

FOR, THE MORE I GROW AND UNDERSTAND
THAT LIFE IS INDEED BOTH RICH AND GRAND,
THE MORE I WANT MY WINGS TO TRY,
AND SOAR AS HIGH AS I CAN FLY

YES, MY LIFE IS CHANGING RAPIDLY,
AND MY "SOUL" DESIRE IS JUST TO BE
TO MY SHINING SELF, EXTREMELY TRUE,
AND ACCOMPLISH ALL WE CAME TO DO

BUT FIRST I KNOW THAT I MUST LEARN
TO TRUST MY SELF AND NOT TO YEARN,
TO HAVE FAITH THAT EACH EXPERIENCE
IS NEEDED AND HELPS ME GROW LESS "DENSE"

12-2-1987

GOD'S LAW OF LOVE STATES: "....WHAT YOU SAY OR DO TO YOUR BRETHREN, YOU SIMULTANEOUSLY SAY OR DO TO YOUR BELOVED SELF...."

"ONE MORE GIFT"

FOR THOSE OF US WHO WISH TO SERVE,
WE'RE ONLY LIMITED BY OUR VERVE;
THIS FACT BECAME QUITE CLEAR, YOU SEE,
AS I PONDERED THE NEXT LIGHT STEP FOR ME

I LEARNED A LESSON THIS YEAR PAST
ON HOW TO LOVE MY SELF THE BEST;
AN ACT OF KINDNESS ON MY PART
FANNED THE FLAME WITHIN MY HEART

WHENE'ER MY GUIDANCE I DID HEED,
THE RESULT WOULD BE A GOD-LIKE DEED;
WHETHER NOTES OF THANKS OR POEMS OF JOY,
THEY WERE TO MY SOUL AN UPLIFTING BUOY

ONE THING I SAW WHILE THIS TOOK PLACE,
YES, THEY PUT A SMILE UPON MY FACE,
BUT THE EARLY DEEDS WERE A BLINDING LIGHT,
WHICH SOON ACCUSTOMED DID MY SIGHT

THIS CAUSED, AT FIRST, IN ME A START;
HOW MANY GIFTS DWELT IN MY HEART?
THE ANSWER CAME LIKE A LION'S ROAR:
WITH GOD, MY CHILD, THERE'S ALWAYS ONE MORE!

12-21-1987

IN THE MOVIE "THELMA AND LOUISE", UPON HEARING THELMA'S COMPLAINT ABOUT HER INSENSITIVE HUSBAND, LOUISE SAYS: "...YOU GET WHAT YOU SETTLE FOR..."

"OPTIONS"

THIS CANTICLE IS OF TWO DIFFERENT BROTHERS
WHO CAME UPON EARTH, BOTH, POWERFUL SOULS,
TO SHOW EVERYONE THAT EACH HAS THEIR 'DRUTHERS,
BY CHOOSING TO WORK TOWARDS OPPOSITE GOALS

THEY LIVED ON EITHER END OF THE TOWN
IN HOMES DISTINGUISHED BY MORE THAN MILES,
THE ONE WITH THE MANSION SEEMED BORN WITH A FROWN,
WHILE THE OTHER, IN HIS HOVEL, HAD A GENTLE SMILE

THEY'D AWAKEN EACH MORNING TO GREET THE DAWN,
THEIR DAYS BEGINNING ON DIVERGENT FEET,
THE MAGNATE COULD BARELY STIFLE A YAWN
BUT, THE PEASANT WAS EAGER THE SUN TO GREET

THROUGHOUT THE DAY, THEY'D PERFORM THEIR TASKS
WITH A FERVOR BEFITTING EACH ONE'S PLACE,
THE BOSS WAS BESIEGED BY MANY WHO ASKED,
WHILE THE PEON TOILED WITH EFFORTLESS GRACE

WHEN THEY FOUND TIME FOR "IDLE" THOUGHTS,
EACH WOULD REFLECT UPON HIS STORY,
THE WORLDLY ONE QUESTIONED WHAT HE HATH WROUGHT,
WHERE THE SIMPLER PRAISED HIS CREATOR'S GLORY

THE CHOICES ARE NEITHER WRONG NOR RIGHT,
FOR THIS IS WHY WE CAME TO EARTH:
TO TREAD THE PATH BACK TO "THE LIGHT"
AND REDISCOVER OUR TRUE WORTH

12-31-1987

HOW ENLIGHTENED WAS OUR BROTHER
WILLIAM (WILL of IAM) SHAKESPEARE (SHAKE the SPEAR)
WHEN HE SAID: "…ALL THE WORLD'S A STAGE…"?

COSMIC SOAP OPERA

IF WE TRULY CREATE ALL THAT WE FEEL,
FROM JOY AND SORROW, TO PLEASURE AND PAIN,
AND IF EVERYTHING IS IN GOD'S GOOD ORDER,
THEN WE NEEDN'T FEEL COMPELLED TO EXPLAIN

THIS HURDLE STILL ELUDES MY LEAP,
AS I JOURNEY THROUGH BOTH TIME AND SPACE,
OFTEN FORGETTING THAT WE'RE ALL PERFORMERS,
I GET TOO CAUGHT UP IN THIS ILLUSORY RACE

I MUST REMEMBER TO BEAR IN MIND
THAT WE'RE SOMETIMES ACTORS IN THE SAME DRAMA,
AND THOUGH THE ANGUISH APPEARS TO BE REAL,
IN TRUTH, WE'RE MOST LIKELY SETTLING SOME KARMA

TO VIEW IT THIS WAY IS HEALTHY INDEED,
FOR NOT ONLY DOES IT ALL EXPLAIN,
IT ALSO ALLOWS A SORT OF DETACHMENT
THAT KEEPS US FROM WALLOWING IN THE PAIN

SO, WHENEVER I FEEL A NEED TO STRESS
WHY SOMEONE SHOULDN'T GET TOO TENSE,
I'LL PICTURE MY self IN "DAYS OF OUR LIVES",
AND HAVE A GOOD LAUGH AT MY OWN EXPENSE

1-02-1988

HOW SWEET OF AN APPLE TO GIVE SUCH A DELICIOUS INTERPRETATION OF.....BODY, MIND AND SPIRIT

"SEPARATION"

"IF GOD IS TRULY A PART OF ME,
THEN I CANNOT BE APART FROM GOD"

THIS FEELS TRUE TO ME, BUT LATELY,
THE THOUGHT OF BEING SEPARATE FROM,
VERSUS "BEING " A PART OF, ALL THAT IS,
CONTINUES TO SEEP INTO MY CURRENT BELIEFS

IF IT IS TRUE THAT GOD CREATED ME
IN HIS/HER /ITS PERFECT IMAGE WITH EVERYTHING
THAT I NEED NOW AND FOR ETERNITY,
THEN WHERE DO MY PHYSICAL
AND ASTRAL BODIES FIT INTO MY PICTURE OF
WHO AND WHAT I REALLY AM?

I KEEP SEEING A HUGE, ANCIENT APPLE TREE
THAT HAS BEEN BEARING FRUIT
SINCE THE BEGINNING OF TIME ON EARTH...
THE ESSENCE OF THAT TREE IS WITHIN
EACH OF ITS VAST NUMBER OF SEEDS
WHICH CAN "GROW" INTO SMALLER TREES

THE FRUIT THAT IS BORNE INCLUDES
A TEMPORAL OUTER LAYER AND A JUICY PULP,
WITH A SEED THAT IS IDENTICAL TO THE ORIGINAL...
ALL THREE PARTS COMPRISE THE WHOLE APPLE
AND ARE CONNECTED TO EACH OTHER
WITH THE ETERNAL, GOD-LIKE SEED AT THE CORE

1-07-1988

BELOVED MASTER MERLIN ONCE SHARED: "....GOD ENLIVENS THE SOUL, AND THE SOUL ENLIVENS THE PERSONALITY..."...IT SEEMS TO ME THAT IT'S ALL GOD!

"APPLES AND ORANGES"

THERE'S A POINT THAT SEEMS TO BE ADDRESSED
WHENE'ER I LEAST EXPECT IT,
AND IT PUTS MY CREDO TO THE TEST,
TO ENSURE I STILL BELIEVE IT

IT HAS TO DO WITH OUR TRUE SELVES,
VERSUS WHO WE THINK WE ARE,
FOR I SOMETIMES SEE ME AS THIS SHELL
THAT HOUSES GOD'S LIGHT, SHINING STAR

I ASKED THE UNIVERSE FOR A TRUTH
TO HELP SEE WHAT'S RIGHT FOR ME,
IT SAID: LIKEN MYSELF TO A PIECE OF FRUIT
THAT'S FROM THE COSMIC TREE

I PICTURED AN APPLE WITH BRIGHT, RED SKIN,
AND A SUCCULENT PULP BENEATH,
WITH ITS TRUE ESSENCE DEEPER WITHIN,
IN THE FORM OF THE PERFECT SEED

IT DIDN'T MATTER IF THE SKIN WAS BRUISED
OR THAT THE PULP WAS SLIGHTLY BITTER,
FOR THESE THINGS WERE OF TEMPORAL USE,
WHILE THE SEED WOULD LAST FOREVER

I SUDDENLY GRASPED MY TRINITY,
THE BODY-MIND, SPIRIT AND SOUL,
BY SEEING MYSELF AS THE FRUIT OF GOD'S TREE
THAT NEEDS ALL THREE PARTS, TO BE WHOLE

1-08-1988

BELOVED GRANDMA "NONNI", WHEN THIS 5 YEAR OLD SAID HE HAD "TO GO" TO THE BATHROOM, ANSWERED: "...WELL GO AHEAD, MICHAEL, NO ONE CAN DO IT FOR YOU..."

"SOLE RESPONSIBILITY"

WHEN WE FIRST CAME UPON THE EARTH,
TO ATTEND HER VARIOUS SCHOOLS,
WE RECEIVED A LESSON QUITE EARLY ON,
AND IT'S ONE OF THE CARDINAL RULES

WHILE OUR MOTHERS CHANGED OUR DIAPERS,
WHICH WE SOILED WHENE'ER WE FELT,
THE MESSAGE WAS THEN QUITE OBVIOUS,
THAT WE HAD "TO GO" OURSELVES

AND SO THIS TRUTH CONTINUED,
AS WE TOOK OUR BABY STEPS,
DESPITE OUR FREQUENT STUMBLINGS,
NO ONE ELSE COULD PASS THE TEST

WE MADE OUR WAY FROM TOT TO TEEN,
ALONE, WE WALKED, THEN LEARNED TO DRIVE,
AND NOW, WE MAY HAVE REACHED THE POINT,
WHERE WE QUESTION THE REASON WE'RE ALIVE

WE EACH MIGHT SENSE A DIFFERENT ANSWER,
THAT SPELLS OUT WHY WE'RE HERE,
THE COMMON FACTOR WITHIN EACH ONE:
TO SHOW GOD'S LOVE, THAT'S FREE FROM FEAR

THEREFORE, AS WE PREPARE OURSELVES
TO TAKE THE FINAL TEST,
REMEMBERING NATURE'S EARLY LESSON,
LET'S GIVE IT OUR VERY BEST!

1-08-1988

THE KORAN, WHICH IS THE MUSLIM HOLY BOOK, SAYS THAT "... GOD IS CLOSER TO YOU THAN THE VEINS IN YOUR NECK..."

"TRUST"

PUTTING ONE'S LIFE INTO THE SOUL'S HANDS,
IS MORE THAN JUST A STATEMENT,
IT REQUIRES THE BEING TO FULLY UNDERSTAND,
THAT IT CALLS FOR THE ego's ABATEMENT

THERE'S A MESSAGE BEING SENT THIS YEAR,
THAT APPLIES FROM THIS DAY HENCE,
TO HEED IT IS TO VANQUISH FEAR,
FOR IT SAYS TO "GET OFF THE FENCE"

IF ONE TRULY BELIEVES THAT THE SOUL IS THEIR GUIDE
ON THIS MOST ONE-DROUS JOURNEY OF ALL,
THEN, TUNE INTO THE VOICE FROM DEEP INSIDE,
AND NEVER BE AFRAID TO FALL

FOR, SUDDENLY THE PATH IS CRYSTAL CLEAR,
WITH NARY A HINT OF CONFUSION,
KNOWING THAT GOD IS ALWAYS NEAR,
SEPARATES THE TRUTH FROM ILLUSION

NO MATTER THE OBSTACLES IN OUR WAY,
ASK NOT FOR THEIR PREVENTION,
SINCE ALONE WE DON'T THE DRAGONS SLAY,
THINK: FORWARD! AND NOT CIRCUMVENTION

THIS PACT MAY CAUSE SOME TO FEEL A BIT NERVOUS,
THAT THEY'VE RELINQUISHED ALL FREE WILL,
BUT IF THEIR DESIRE IS TRULY FOR SERVICE,
THEN THE FIRST DEMON HAS JUST BEEN KILLED

1-12-1988

THE BARD WAS "RIGHT ON" AGAIN, AS USUAL…"…PARTING IS SUCH SWEET SORROW…."

"AU REVOIR"

AS THE DAYS GO BY, THE MORE AM I
TO MY GOD-LIKE SELF SO TRUE,
THIS OFT IMPLIES, SOME PAINFUL GOODBYES,
FOR THOSE TO WHOM THIS IS NEW

FOR NOW IS THE TIME, WHEN THE TRUTH, I FIND,
REACHES RIGHT DOWN TO MY CORE,
AND THE WAY THINGS WERE, SEEM SUCH A BLUR,
THEY'RE NOT RIGHT FOR ME ANYMORE

THOSE WHO SAY, THEY LOVED THE WAY,
I WAS BEFORE MY "STRANGE SHIFT",
CANNOT RELATE, OR EVEN TOLERATE,
THE THINGS THAT, TO ME, ARE A GIFT

I FACE A TRIP, FOR WHICH I'M EQUIPPED,
WHILE THE OTHERS ARE STILL IN A QUAND'RY,
AND IF I CHOOSE TO WAIT, OR EVEN HESITATE,
THEN, THE TRAIN WILL LEAVE WITHOUT ME

ALTHOUGH I CARE, I'M WELL AWARE,
THAT WE EACH HAVE OUR OWN LIFE MISSION,
WHICH CAN ONLY BE DONE, BY THE DAUGHTER OR SON,
WHO WAS GIVEN THE COMMISSION

SO, TO ALL WHO GRIEVE, AND DON'T BELIEVE,
THE TRUTHS THAT I'VE EMBRACED,
IT'S REALLY OKAY, AND THERE'LL COME THE DAY,
WHEN WE'RE, ONCE AGAIN, FACE TO FACE

1-13-1988

IT'S BEEN SAID THAT…"…WHEN AN ENTITY REACHES THE OUTER EDGE OF THEIR "COMFORT ZONE"….THEREIN BEGINS TRUE LIVING…."

"PIONEERS"

THIS IS A SONG FOR US PIONEERS
WHO BLAZE THE TRAIL OF LIGHT,
ALTHOUGH OUR TASK IS SOMEWHAT LONELY,
WE GIVE IT ALL OUR MIGHT

WE'RE UNAFRAID TO TAKE THE RISKS
THAT OFT LEAD TO RIDICULE,
FOR, WHILE IT APPEARS WE'RE SOMEWHAT STRANGE,
TO GOD, WE'RE FAR FROM FOOLS

SPOUSES AND CHILDREN CANNOT EXPLAIN
THE THINGS THAT THEY NOW SEE,
AND THE MORE THEY RESIST THEIR LOVED ONE'S GROWTH,
THE MORE DETERMINED IS HE OR SHE

FOR WHAT ELSE CAN WE WORKERS DO,
ONCE THE COMMITMENT HAS BEEN MADE,
SERVICE TO GOD IS OUR PURPOSE NOW,
WITH LOVE AND JOY OUR STOCK IN TRADE

WE'VE GIVEN UP TRYING TO EXPLAIN
WHY WE FEEL THE WAY WE DO,
MOST PEOPLE AREN'T READY TO HEAR
THAT WE'RE JUST BEING, TO OUR GOD-SELF, TRUE

THERE'S A COSMIC CONSOLATION IN THIS,
AND IT'S COMFORTING TO HEAR,
SOME DAY ALL WILL TREAD THE GOLDEN PATH
THAT WE HELPED PIONEER!

1-15-1988

"A COURSE IN MIRACLES" HAS A LESSON WHICH STATES: "...I WILL STEP BACK AND LET HIM LEAD THE WAY..." BELOVED MASTER MERLIN PUT IT A LITTLE DIFFERENTLY: "...EXCUSE ONESELF FROM THE PERSONALITY..."

"GOING WITH THE FLOW"

HOW OFTEN HAS YOUR SENSE OF FRUSTRATION
MADE YOU WANT TO "CHUCK IT" ALL,
WHETHER A JOB, A FRIEND OR RELATIONSHIP,
IT'S LIKE BEATING YOUR HEAD AGAINST THE WALL

TRY AS YOU MAY TO CONFORM AND ADAPT,
NOTHING SEEMS TO FEEL JUST RIGHT,
THIS APPARENTLY IS PART OF OUR SPECIAL JOURNEY
OF RETURNING HOME, BACK TO THE LIGHT

FOR, IF AS ABOVE, SO TOO BELOW,
AND LIGHT INDEED ATTRACTS THE LIGHT,
THEN IT'S MERELY A MATTER OF NO LONGER MESHING,
WITH THAT WHICH ONCE WAS A SATISFACTORY LIFE

THE ANSWER TO THIS, IS NOT TO RESIST,
OUR LIFE'S DIVINELY GUIDED FLOW,
AND WHEN WE ENCOUNTER A SNAG OR A BLOCKAGE,
RELAX, HAVE FAITH, AND SIMPLY LET GO

WE ALL ARE PART OF THE HANDS OF GOD,
WHO ONLY WANTS THE VERY BEST FOR US,
SO, THE NEXT TIME YOU FEEL THAT OLD FRUSTRATION,
TAKE A DEEP BREATH, AND GIVE HER YOUR TRUST

1-20-1988

MORE THAN TWENTY YEARS AFTER FIRST MEETING MY BELOVED MASTER MERLIN, I STILL FEEL SO INCREDIBLY BLESSED FOR THE FIVE YEARS WE SPENT TOGETHER

"MERLIN"

THE DAY I CHANGED MY LIFE FOREVER,
I RECEIVED A MESSAGE, BOTH WISE AND TRUE,
MY MASTER EXPLAINED MANY CONCEPTS TO ME,
THE MOST PROFOUND WAS: "YOU 'VE A RIGHT TO BE YOU"

HAVING RAISED A FAMILY MOST OF MY LIFE,
WITH ALL THE TRIALS, AND EVEN MORE JOYS,
I MUST ADMIT I WAS SOMEWHAT CONFUSED,
BY THE WORDS SPOKEN THROUGH DIANA'S VOICE

I HAD NEVER GIVEN MUCH THOUGHT TO ME,
SINCE I HAD FOUR OTHERS TO CARE ABOUT,
I WAS TAUGHT TO ALWAYS PUT MYSELF LAST,
FOR, DOING ELSEWISE WOULD MAKE ME A LOUSE

BUT, HE WASN'T SPEAKING OF ego *WANTS,*
WHEN HE TALKED OF PUTTING MY "SELF" FIRST,
IT WAS SPIRITUAL GROWTH THAT WAS STRESSED BY HIM,
AND THE REASON I REALLY CAME TO EARTH

TO CLINCH THE MESSAGE, HE GAVE ME A SIGN,
AND TOLD ME SOMETHING THAT NO ONE ELSE KNEW,
THIS STRUCK A CHORD DEEP DOWN IN MY SOUL,
FOR, I KNEW, RIGHT THEN, THAT THE WORDS WERE TRUE

THIS HAPPENED OVER A YEAR AGO,
SO MUCH HAS CHANGED WITH THE PASSAGE OF TIME,
THIS PAEAN IS FOR MY BELOVED MASTER,
WHO TAPPED MY SHOULDER, AND SAID I COULD FLY

1-27-1988

SWEET PEARL LOVED TO REMIND ALL OF US: "…THERE ARE NO ACCIDENTS…..EVAH!…."

"DIVINE ORDER"

SINCE REALIZING I AM THE HANDS OF GOD,
AND TRULY KNOWING THIS TO BE SO,
THERE'S NEVER A PROBLEM THAT SEEMS VERY HARD,
BECAUSE I CHOOSE TO GO WITH THE FLOW

EACH DAY, THIS CHOICE FEELS BETTER AND BETTER,
AS MY "OLD WORLD" RESISTANCE EBBS AND WANES,
I FOLLOW MY PRECEPT TO THE LETTER,
AND SPARE MYSELF SOME NEEDLESS PAIN

FOR, I BELIEVE THERE ARE NO MISTAKES,
HOW CAN THERE BE IN THE COSMIC MIND?
AND, EACH OF US, NOW, IS IN THE RIGHT PLACE,
WHETHER OR NOT WE BELIEVE THAT LINE

THE JOBS WE HAVE, AND THE PEOPLE WE MEET,
ARE NEEDED TO HELP US LEARN AND GROW,
IF WE SAVOR EACH DAY, LIKE A SPECIAL TREAT,
WE'LL SEE THAT EVERYTHING IS MEANT TO SHOW

SO, DON'T RESIST WHAT'S HAPPENING NOW,
RATHER, GIVE IT ALL YOUR BENEDICTION,
OF COURSE, FREE WILL IS ALWAYS ALLOWED,
THE CHOICE IS EITHER FLUENCY OR…..FRICTION

1-27-1988

IT'S BEEN SAID THAT GOD'S MIND IS THE RIVER OF THOUGHT… WHERE THE THOUGHT IS LOWERED INTO LIGHT, AND THEN THE LIGHT IS LOWERED INTO ELECTRICAL IMPULSES WHICH ARE LOWERED INTO MASS, WHICH IS LOWERED TO REPRESENT THE THOUGHT IDEAL

"THE RIVER"

OFTIMES, I GET AN INSPIRATION,
FROM THE STAR THAT'S DEEP WITHIN MY HEART,
WHENE'ER I DO, THERE'S NO HESITATION,
FOR, IT'S GOD'S SIGNAL FOR ME TO START

IT DOESN'T MATTER WHAT I'M ASKED TO DO,
THE DEEDS ARE ALL THE SAME TO ME,
MY GOAL IS THE TOTAL INTEGRATION,
OF THE THREE PARTS OF MY TRINITY

WE WORK TOGETHER, AS A TEAM,
DOING GOD'S WORK FOR ALL TO SEE,
MY SHINING STAR SENDS THE THOUGHT TO MY SOUL,
WHO THEN JUST PASSES IT ON TO ME

THE IMPULSES TAKE SO MANY FORMS,
FROM POEMS LIKE THESE, TO ACTS OF LOVE,
THEIR SOURCE DOES NOT BEGIN ON EARTH,
THEY'RE CHANNELED FROM WAY UP ABOVE

I PICTURE THIS LIKE A MIGHTY RIVER,
THAT SPANS THE PLANET FROM NORTH TO SOUTH,
EACH DROP OF WATER THAT COURSES ITS LENGTH,
COMES FROM THE SOURCE AT THE RIVER'S MOUTH

THIS HELPS ME UNDERSTAND IT MORE, EXCEPT,
IT'S NOT A BODY OF WATER, RAGING,
I SEE IT, RATHER, AS A RIVER OF LIGHT,
WITH ME AS ONE OF ITS PUMPING STATIONS

1-31-1988

AFTER 20 YEARS, BELOVED MASTER MERLIN'S WORDS: "...YOU'RE NOT RESPONSIBLE FOR OTHERS' RESPONSES TO YOU...THEY MUST TAKE CREDIT FOR WHAT THEY ARE, TOO...", ARE STILL TOUGH TO LIVE AT TIMES

"RESPONSE ABILITY"

MY MASTER TAUGHT ME MANY THINGS,
THAT FATEFUL DAY , A YEAR AGO,
HE SPOKE OF THE PEACE THAT PATIENCE BRINGS,
WHEN YOU TRUST IN YOUR SELF, AND JUST LET GO

HE STRESSED A POINT QUITE NEW TO ME,
AS ALL THEY WERE THAT SPECIAL DAY,
HE SAID I BORE NO RESPONSIBILITY,
FOR THE WAY PEOPLE REACT TO WHAT I MIGHT SAY

BEING A TYPE TO CAUSE NO PAIN,
THIS WAS HARD FOR ME TO SWALLOW,
I'VE SPENT MY LIFE TRYING TO EXPLAIN,
ALL MY MOTIVES, WHETHER DEEP OR SHALLOW

HE SAID IT WAS MY JOB TO ALWAYS DISCERN,
ALL THAT OCCURRED THROUGHOUT THE DAY,
IT WAS UP TO ME TO HEED AND LEARN,
IF I WAS UPSET BY WHAT SOMEONE WOULD SAY

THE SAME IS TRUE FOR ANY SOUL,
WHO MAY NOT LIKE WHAT I DO OR SAY,
SINCE EACH OF US HAS THE VERY SAME GOAL,
OF KNOWING OUR SELVES, IN EVERY WAY

THIS WISDOM ALLOWS ME TO TRULY BE "ME",
AS LONG AS HURTING IS NOT MY DESIRE,
EXPRESSING MY "SELF", LIKE A BIRD THAT'S BEEN FREED,
AND STOKING THE FURNACE OF GOD'S GOLDEN FIRE

2-04-1988

PARAMAHANSA YOGANANDA TAUGHT: "...WITHIN YOU LIES THE SEA OF INFINITE KNOWLEDGE AND INSPIRATION..."

"SOLUTIONS"

FOR ALL LIFE'S PROBLEMS, THERE IS A CLUE,
THAT HELPS TO SHOW US WHAT TO DO,
WHEN THE ANSWER APPEARS TO BE ELUSIVE,
REMEMBER, THAT FEELING IS MERELY ILLUSIVE

HOW OFTEN HAS A RIDDLE BEEN POSED TO YOU,
AND YOU'D SCRATCH YOUR HEAD, THINKING IT THROUGH,
UPON HEARING THE ANSWER, YOU'D MAKE A FUSS,
WHEN YOU REALIZED HOW SIMPLE THE PROCESS WAS

OFTIMES, WE WASTE MUCH ENERGY,
ON THE PROBLEM THAT WE ALREADY SEE,
THIS ONLY CAUSES LOTS MORE CONFUSION,
FOR, 'TIS BETTER TO FOCUS ON THE SOLUTION

AS WITH THE RIDDLE, THE ANSWER EXISTS,
AND IF WE STILL CAN'T FIGURE IT,
RELAX, STAY CALM, AND GO QUIETLY WITHIN,
AND LET YOUR GOD-SELF GLADLY PITCH IN

THIS IS A LESSON WE EACH MUST LEARN,
IF WE TRULY WANT OUR FLAME TO BURN,
ALL OF LIFE'S ANSWERS ARE SIMPLE, LET'S TRUST,
THEY RESIDE, RIGHT NOW, IN EACH OF US

2-07-1988

IN KINDERGARTEN WE LEARNED "....FIRST THINGS FIRST..." HOW TRUE, HOW TRUE

"THE SOURCE"

WHEN CHRIST INSTRUCTED THAT WE LOVE OUR NEIGHBOR,
WITH THE SAME LOVE WE HAVE FOR OUR SELVES,
THE MESSAGE CONTAINED TWO LESSONS TO LEARN,
IF WE SINCERELY WISHED TO GROW AND EXCEL

AS WITH ALL THINGS, WE ARE THE SOURCE,
FROM WHICH SPRINGS FORTH OUR WEALTH,
SO, BEFORE WE CAN TRULY LOVE ANOTHER,
WE MUST FIRSTLY LOVE OUR SELVES

THIS LOVE IS FREE OF ALL CONDITIONS,
WE NURTURE OUR BODY-MIND, SPIRIT AND SOUL,
THINKING AND FEELING ONLY THE BEST,
WE BECOME COMPLETELY WHOLE

WITH THIS FOUNDATION, WE ARE READY TO SERVE,
OUR BROTHERS AND SISTERS ON EARTH,
FOR, WE'LL LOOK UPON EACH ONE OF THEM,
AS BEINGS DESERVING OUR WORTH

THE PEACE WE'LL FEEL, AS WE GROW IN LOVE,
FOR OUR SELVES AND THOSE WE MEET,
WILL ALLOW US TO WALK ALL O'ER THE EARTH,
WITH WINGS UPON OUR FEET

2-11-1988

IS THIS WHAT'S MEANT BY "...SEEK FIRST THE KINGDOM OF HEAVEN WITHIN YOU?"

"GOING HOME"

THERE'S A PLACE INSIDE EACH ONE OF US,
THAT I HAVE LATELY FOUND,
WHERE PEACE AND LOVE DWELL SIDE BY SIDE,
AND TRUST IN SELF ABOUNDS

THIS PLACE WAS NEVER LOST TO ME,
IT WAS MORE OF AN OCCLUSION,
MY GROWING PAINS CAUSED MUCH DISTRACTION,
CREATING GREAT CLOUDS OF CONFUSION

AND SO, I WALKED IN A HEAVY FOG,
NOT SEEING WHAT WAS SO NEAR,
PRAYING THAT GOD WOULD GRANT TO ME,
THE THINGS I HELD SO DEAR

DURING THIS TIME, I LEARNED TO TRUST,
THAT EVERYTHING'S FOR A REASON,
I GLADLY GAVE MY LOVE TO ALL,
THIS PAST CHRISTMAS SEASON

THERE WAS ONE MORE TASK I HAD TO DO,
AND THAT WAS TO RELEASE,
MY ATTACHMENT TO ALL WHICH WAS IN MY LIFE,
THIS DONE, I CAME HOME TO PEACE

2-14-88

SHAKESPEARE WROTE: "…TO THINE OWN SELF BE TRUE…"
BELOVED MASTER MERLIN SAID: "…BE TRUE TO YOUR SELF, OR BE IN PAIN…" BELOVED GANDHI BELIEVED: "…GOD IS TRUTH…"

"TWO SIDES OF LOVE"

PURE LOVE HAS NO CONDITIONS, I FEEL,
WHEN TRULY EXPRESSED, IT'S VERY REAL,
FOR, IT GIVES WITH NO THOUGHT OF RETURN,
CAUSING THE FLAME WITHIN TO BURN

TODAY, "LOVE" HAS MANY FACES AND NAMES,
ALLOWING SOULS TO PLAY THEIR SUBTLE GAMES,
ONE SAYS THAT "LOVE" IS THERE FOR YOU,
PROVIDED YOU DO AS THEY WANT YOU TO

ANOTHER HAS SOME SIMILAR RULES,
THIS ONE PROMISES ALL OF "LOVE'S" JEWELS,
IF ONLY YOU MAKE SOME ALTERATIONS,
TO HABITS THAT, TO THEM, ARE REAL VEXATIONS

THERE'S A PATTERN THAT'S OCCURRING HERE,
THESE "LOVE" GAMES PREY UPON THE FEAR,
OF LOSING THE ONE WHO HOLDS OUR HEART,
IF WE DON'T CONFORM, AND PLAY THE PART

THE QUESTION EACH SOUL MUST SOME DAY ASK,
INQUIRES WHETHER IT'S WORTH THE TASK,
THAT COMPROMISES ONE'S CURRENT VIEW,
AND HINDERS YOU FROM BEING "YOU"

"LOVE" GAMES CREATE A HOST OF CONFUSION,
BECAUSE THAT "LOVE" IS MERELY ILLUSION,
WHILE PURE LOVE'S NATURE IS TO SOOTHE,
FOR, IT COMES FROM GOD, WHO IS "THE TRUTH"

2-15-1988

UNLIKE APPLES, HUMANS MUST CHOOSE TO GROW, OR, AT LEAST MAKE THE FENCE MORE COMFORTABLE

"THE POWER OF LIGHT"

WHEN I QUESTION WHAT I'M HERE TO DO,
AS I CONTINUE MY QUEST FOR ME,
I RECEIVE, FROM WITHIN, AN EASY REPLY,
ONCE AGAIN, TO LOOK AT THE TREE

I SUDDENLY SEE THE SIMPLE TRUTH,
IN A TREE WHOSE FRUIT'S NOT RIPE,
WHERE SOME ARE GREEN AND NEED MORE TIME,
AND OTHERS, JUST A BIT MORE LIGHT

FOR THOSE THAT NEED THE LITTLE PUSH,
OF THE SUNLIGHT'S WARMTH AND POWER,
TO REACH A POINT THAT'S BEAUTIFULLY SWEET,
THEIR TIME IS WITHIN THE HOUR

THE SAME IS TRUE OF ALL GOD'S SOULS,
THAT ADORN HIS EARTHLY TREE,
THERE ARE MANY REQUIRING MORE TIME TO GROW,
AND SOME, WHO ARE READY TO SEE

IT'S THE LATTER GROUP I'M HERE TO ADDRESS,
THIS FEELS, TO ME, VERY RIGHT,
THEIR HEARTS ARE SLOWLY STARTING TO OPE',
AND WELCOME MY WORDS OF LIGHT

AND WHEN THEY FEEL THE TRUTH WITHIN,
ALLOWING THEIR HEARTS TO SENSE,
THE NEW AWARENESS WILL CHANGE THEIR LIVES,
IF THEY CHOOSE TO GET OFF THE FENCE

3-05-1988

A LOVING AND WISE ENTITY ONCE REFERRED TO THE HUMAN SOUL AS A MUTANT…..PART MAN, PART GOD. THE BODY IS THE REFLECTION OF THE SOUL, THE IMAGE, IF YOU WILL. WHEN YOU LOOK INTO YOUR EYES…..DO YOU SEE GOD?

"SELF ESTEEM"

I RECENTLY READ ONE BEING'S TRUTH,
CONCERNING AN ELUSIVE TRAIT,
IT MATTERS NOT WHETHER WE'RE YOUNG OR OLD,
WE ALL SEEM CONTENT TO WAIT

I'M SPEAKING OF SOMETHING THAT'S MOST ESSENTIAL,
IF EVER WE'RE GOING TO FLY,
IT'S OUR OWN IMAGE THAT WE SEE EACH DAY,
AND IT'S STORED IN OUR MIND'S EYE

IF THE PICTURE IS BRIGHT, AND FILLED WITH LOVE,
OUR WORLD WILL LOOK THE SAME,
BUT IF IT'S CLOUDED, CONSUMED WITH GUILT,
THEN, WE'RE PLAYING THE ego's GAME

FOR, AS WE'VE WRITTEN ONCE BEFORE,
EVERYTHING SPRINGS FROM US,
AND IF WE CHOOSE TO HATE OUR SELVES,
THEN, OUR SPIRIT'S SHROUDED IN DUST

THE REFERENCED BEING FEELS THE BUILDING BLOCKS,
REQUIRED TO HELP US GLEAM,
ARE HONESTY, TRUST AND INTEGRITY,
SOME CORNERSTONES OF "SELF" ESTEEM

HE ALSO ADDS TO THE LIST ABOVE,
THE MOST IMPORTANT THING, TO ME,
IN ORDER TO BE EVER TRUE TO OUR SELVES,
WE MUST HAVE "RESPONSE" ABILITY

4-07-1988

THE DAY THIS WAS WRITTEN, I WAS COMING MOSTLY FROM MY PERSONALITY.....LIKE AN ENTITY WITH TWO HEADS THAT WERE BICKERING BACK AND FORTH

"FAITH"

AS I CONTINUE MY QUEST FOR INNER PEACE,
AND THE WHOLENESS WITH GOD IT BRINGS,
I'M LEARNING THAT SOMETHING MUST BE RELEASED,
IF MY SOUL IS TO TRULY SING

ALTHOUGH I TRUST GOD WANTS ONLY THE BEST
IN ALL THINGS THAT I TRY TO DO,
THERE ARE TIMES MY FAITH IS PUT TO THE TEST,
WHEN MY PLANS SEEM TO JUST FALL THROUGH

I KNOW, IN MY SOUL, THERE'S AN INTRICATE PATTERN
OF WHICH I, LIKE YOU, AM A PART,
BUT, WHEN I SEEK TO KNOW WHY SOMETHING "NEGATIVE"
HAPPENED, THEN IT'S MY ego SHUTTING DOWN MY HEART

IF ONE TRULY HAS FAITH, THEN, THERE IS NO NEED
TO KNOW THE WHYS OF ILLUSORY THINGS,
FOR, FAITH BRINGS PEACE, WHICH PROVIDES WITH SPEED,
THE ABILITY TO FLY WITH TRUTH'S WINGS

FOR ME, THE ONLY REALITY
IS GOD'S PRESENCE WITHIN MY SOUL,
WHEN THAT BECOMES THE SOURCE OF ALL THAT I SEE,
THEN, I WILL BE COMPLETELY WHOLE

AND BEING WHOLE, MY LIFE WILL FLOW,
LIKE WATER OFF THE BACK OF A DUCK,
NEVER AGAIN WILL I NEED THE "WHY" TO KNOW,
OR RELY ON THE ILLUSION OF LUCK

5-14-1988

"...AN EYE FOR AN EYE ONLY MAKES THE WHOLE WORLD BLIND...",
"....WE ARE ALL TARRED WITH THE SAME BRUSH...", "...GOD IS
TRUTH...", SOME QUOTES FROM M.K.GANDHI

"GANDHI"

THERE'S A SOUL LIKE WHOM I WANT TO BE,
HIS NAME WAS MOHANDAS K. GANDHI,
HE BELIEVED IN FREEDOM FOR HIS NATION,
AND SAW THROUGH THE SEEMING SEPARATION

HE LOVED THE CREATOR OF ALL THINGS,
AND FOUND THE PEACE THAT TRUSTING BRINGS,
HE KNEW THE LIGHT DWELT IN HIS HEART;
THAT HIS BRETHREN AND HE WERE OF GOD A PART

NE'ER WAS THERE A TIME THAT HE WOULD MISS
A CHANCE TO FIGHT AGAINST INJUSTICE,
THE BATTLES HE WAGED NEITHER HURT NOR KILLED,
HIS ONLY WEAPONS WERE LOVE AND GOD'S WILL

IN HIS DAY, LINES WERE CLEARLY DRAWN,
DEPENDING ON THE LIFE TO WHICH ONE WAS BORN,
SOCIETY FELT THAT WOMEN WERE TOOLS,
AND IT WOULDN'T EMBRACE THE "UNTOUCHABLES"

THESE ATTITUDES WERE WEIGHTS AROUND HIS SOUL,
FOR HE KNEW HIS COUNTRY COULD NEVER BE WHOLE,
UNTIL EACH ONE SAW WHAT WAS CLEAR TO HIM,
AND LEARNED TO LOVE THE GOD WITHIN

GANDHI AND CHRIST, GREAT TEACHERS BOTH,
FOR ME, THEY ARE SHINING BEACONS OF HOPE,
SHOWING THAT WE ALL CAN ATTAIN SUCH HEIGHTS,
IF WE TRULY DESIRE TO LIVE IN "THE LIGHT"

6-05-1988

THIS EVENT WAS HELD AT THE LOS ANGELES COLISEUM, WITH AN EXPECTED CROWD OF 100,000. THE STADIUM WAS EMPTY EXCEPT FOR ONE END ZONE, BUT I WROTE THIS POEM FOR THE OCCASION

"AWAKENING"

I WAS INSPIRED TO WRITE THIS SONG TODAY,
ON THE EVE OF A GREAT EVENT,
WHICH HOPES TO RELEASE OUR WORLDLY WAYS,
AND REMIND US WE'RE HEAVEN SENT

IT'S BEEN DUBBED: "STARLINK '88",
TO SHOW THE INTERCONNECTION,
BETWEEN US EXISTING IN TIME AND SPACE,
AND THOSE IN THE FOURTH DIMENSION

TOO LONG WE'VE WANDERED IN OUR SLEEP,
FORGETTING FROM WHENCE WE CAME,
BELIEVING ONLY WHAT OUR EYES COULD SEE,
AND LOOKING FOR SOMEONE TO BLAME

WE'D PASS A SOUL WALKING DOWN THE STREET,
UNAWARE OF THE SHINING STAR,
THAT GLOWED IN SYNC WITH EACH HEARTBEAT,
THE "SOLE" TRUTH OF WHO WE ARE

IN ORDER TO HELP COMPLETE GOD'S PLAN,
WHICH CALLS FOR HEAVEN ON EARTH,
THEN, IT'S TIME, RIGHT NOW, EACH WOMAN AND MAN,
TO ACKNOWLEDGE OUR TRUE WORTH

THE NEW AGE HAS BEEN CALLED THE TIME
WHEN WE SUCCESSFULLY INTEGRATE,
THE ENERGIES OF THE SPIRIT, SOUL AND MIND,
WELCOME HOME! LOVE, "STARLINK '88"

6-08-1988

EAT, DRINK AND MAKE MERRY.....JUST GIVE YOUR TRUE SELF A FAIR SHAKE

"PURIFICATION I"

I'M LEARNING IF WE WANT TO FAN THE FIRE
OF GOD'S FLAME WITHIN OUR ETERNAL SOUL,
IT'S A MUST TO CURB OUR PHYSICAL DESIRES,
WHICH KEEP US FROM BEING COMPLETELY WHOLE

THESE CARNAL QUIRKS HAVE MANY FORMS,
FROM OVEREATING TO WANTON LUST,
THEY MANAGE TO TAKE OUR PASSIONS BY STORM,
WITH OUR ego *SAYING THEY ARE A MUST*

SINCE OUR EARTHLY BODIES NEED TO BE FED,
AND SEEK BRIEF COMFORT IN BLENDING WITH ANOTHER,
WE MUST STRIVE TO NEGATE THE TURMOIL THAT'S BRED,
AND KEEPS US FROM SERVING OUR ROUSING BROTHERS

FOR, IF WE CANNOT MASTER SIMPLE CONTROL
OVER THESE ILLUSORY THINGS OF THE TEMPORAL FLESH,
THEN, WE'LL NEVER BE COMPLETELY WHOLE,
'CAUSE OUR BODIES AND SOULS CAN'T EVER MESH

I BELIEVE WE'RE HERE TO MANIFEST
THE PERFECTION THAT DWELLS WITHIN OUR SOULS,
TO DO THAT, WE MUST PASS ALL THE TESTS
WHICH LEAD TO THE HIGHEST HEAVENLY GOALS

WHEN TEMPTED TO YIELD TO INSATIABLE DESIRE,
PAY HEED TO YOUR ALL WISE, SHINING STAR,
WHO ONLY WANTS YOU TO FLY YET HIGHER,
AND SHOW GOD'S SONS WHO THEY REALLY ARE

6-24-1988

THE BEST THINGS IN LIFE REALLY ARE FREE!

"IT'S A GREAT LIFE"

WHEN I STEP OUTSIDE IN THE EARLY MORN',
SMELLING AND FEELING THE CLEAN, COOL AIR,
I SENSE OUR FATHER'S PRESENCE AROUND ME,
AND I THINK TO MYSELF: "IT'S A GREAT LIFE!"

AS I SIT AT THE TABLE, ENJOYING MY MEAL,
AND WATCH ALL THE BIRDS DO THE SAME,
I FEEL THE CONNECTION THAT ALL OF US SHARE,
AND SING TO MYSELF: "IT'S A GREAT LIFE!"

AS I APPROACH THE DOORWAY THAT LEADS TO MY TRADE,
SEEING THE TREES, THE BEES AND THE WATER ABOUT,
I'M GRATEFUL TO WORK NEAR SUCH SIMPLE BEAUTY,
SO, I SAY, ONCE AGAIN: "IT'S A GREAT LIFE!"

AS I SMILE AT A "STRANGER" I PASS ON THE STAIRS,
SURPRISING THEM INTO A PLEASANT "GOOD MORNING",
IT'S EASY TO SEE THERE'S NO SEPARATION,
AND I FEEL MORE STRONGLY: "IT'S A GREAT LIFE!"

WHEN I ENCOUNTER A SOUL NOT SEEN IN AWHILE,
AND WE SHARE SOME WORDS THAT BOOST EACH OF US UP,
I'M REMINDED, ONCE MORE, THERE'S NO CHANCE OF "CHANCE",
AND I WANT TO SHOUT ALOUD: "IT'S A GREAT LIFE!"

AS I WALK AT NIGHT, WITH THE MOON AND THE STARS,
SEEING MY HEAVENLY BROTHERS AND SISTERS ABOVE,
I KNOW THAT I'M A PART OF "ALL THAT IS",
AND THE VOICE WITHIN AUMS: "IT'S A GREAT LIFE!"

6-24-1988

OF ALL THE PEOPLE IN MY LIFE THAT HAD PASSED ON, JACKIE GLEASON WAS THE FIRST ONE, UPON HEARING OF HIS PASSING, THAT I WEPT FOR....I REALLY LOVED "RALPHIE BOY"

"THE GREAT ONE"

TODAY MARKS THE FIRST ANNIVERSARY,
OF THE PASSING OF A SOUL WHO WAS DEAR TO ME,
HIS HEART WAS AS LARGE AS HIS SIZEABLE GIRTH,
GIVING HIS ALL, IF HE FELT THE WORTH

HE HAD MANY FACES TO SHOW ME AND YOU,
FROM MAKING US LAUGH, TO TWIRLING A CUE,
IF ANYTHING BORE HIS PERSONAL SIGN,
YOU'D BE SURE OF ENJOYING A WONDERFUL TIME

HE ALSO MADE MUSIC, WAY BACK WHEN,
BEFORE THE WORLD KNEW OF HIS TALENTS AND KEN,
BUT THE CHARACTER MOST PEOPLE CHUCKLE ABOUT,
WAS A LOVEABLE LOUDMOUTH, WHOSE FIRST NAME WAS RALPH

AS CHARACTERS GO, RALPH WAS MISUNDERSTOOD,
FOR, BENEATH THE FACADE, DWELT A SOUL THAT WAS GOOD,
HE'D BELLOW AND ROAR, AND STOMP ALL ABOUT,
PROJECTING TO MOST, AN INSENSITIVE LOUT

IF PEOPLE HAD TAKEN THE TIME TO DISCERN,
THEY'D HAVE SEEN A SMALL LESSON WE ALL NEED TO LEARN,
FOR RALPH, LIKE JACKIE, HAD A HEART OF GOLD,
BUT IT TOOK QUITE AWHILE FOR IT TO UNFOLD

THIS GIANT WAS LIKE MUCH OF THE WORLD TODAY,
PROJECTING AN IMAGE OF THE OPPOSITE WAY,
THE HEARTS OF MILLIONS TRULY YEARN TO BE,
REVEALING GOD'S STAR, FOR MANKIND TO SEE

6-24-1988

BELOVED MASTER JESUS ONCE SAID: "…WHAT YOU DO FOR THE LEAST OF MY BRETHREN, YOU DO FOR ME…"

"SHARING"

WE'VE WRITTEN TIME AND TIME AGAIN,
THAT THE HIGHEST WAY TO PEACE AND JOY,
IS THROUGH THE STAR WITHIN OUR HEARTS,
THAT TIES US TO THE WORLD ON HIGH

WHILE I FEEL THE TRUTH OF THAT REMARK,
IN HONESTY, I MUST CONFESS,
THAT SHARING ONE'S LIFE WITH KINDRED SOULS,
TAKES SOMETHING GOOD, AND MAKES IT "BEST"

I CAN SIT ALONE AND WATCH THE SUN
AS IT "DISAPPEARS" IN THE DEEP, BLUE SEA,
FEELING CONNECTED TO "ALL THAT IS",
WHETHER OR NOT SOMEONE'S WITH ME

BUT, IF I ACCOMPLISH A MAJOR TASK,
OR WANT TO SHARE MY FEELINGS TRUE,
THEN, IT'S GREAT TO HAVE A SOUL NEARBY
WHO LOOKS AT LIFE THE WAY I DO

GOD'S LAW OF LOVE MAKES NO DISTINCTION
'TWEEN GIVING AND RECEIVING; THAT'S DIVINELY FAIR,
THIS FACT PROVIDES ME WITH THE REASON
WHY EVERYTHING'S TWICE AS NICE WHEN SHARED

AND SO, I'LL SHARE MY SELF WITH OTHERS,
OFFERING THEM MY VERY BEST,
SINCE I BELIEVE WE'RE LINKED TOGETHER,
THERE'S NO NEED TO SEPARATE ONE FROM THE REST

6-29-1988

THE ONLY CAGE THAT CAN EVER IMPRISON US IS THE ILLUSORY ONE MADE BY OUR ego's

"TRUE FREEDOM"

IT'S TIME TO SHED SOME LIGHT ON A "THING"
THAT, UP 'TIL NOW, WAS REALLY A SHADOW,
APPEARING TO BE A BRIGHT, BRASS RING,
BUT SHOWING, AGAIN, MY PERCEPTIONS WERE NARROW

IT SEEMED THAT ALL I'D EVER NEED,
TO TRULY SPREAD MY WINGS AND FLY,
WAS MY OWN SPACE, WHERE I COULD PROCEED
TO MOVE ALL ABOUT, AND NOT EXPLAIN WHY

THIS WOULD PROVIDE THE JAILER'S KEY,
FOR ALL THE RESTRICTIONS, IN MY MIND,
AFTER SO MANY YEARS, I'D FINALLY BE "FREE",
AT THE COST OF LEAVING MY LOVED ONES BEHIND

AND THEN, I THOUGHT OF SOME PEOPLE I KNOW,
WHO SEEMED TO HAVE WHAT I HELD MOST DEAR,
YES, THEY LIVED ALONE, AND COULD COME AND GO,
BUT STILL, THEY WERE GRIPPED BY WORLDLY FEARS

THEY SOUGHT FOR "THINGS" TO MAKE THEM GLAD,
LIKE MONEY, FAME AND RELATIONSHIPS TOO,
AND YET, THEIR EYES APPEARED SO SAD,
BECAUSE THESE "THINGS" WERE NOT REAL OR TRUE

I KNOW, IN MY HEART, THERE IS NO FEAR,
AND NO "THING" CAN EITHER HELP OR HURT,
AS LONG AS I KEEP MY PERCEPTIONS CLEAR,
I'M AS FREE AND HAPPY AS A SOARING BIRD

7-17-1988

"...HE WHO PERCEIVES ME EVERYWHERE, AND BEHOLDS EVERYTHING IN ME, NEVER LOSES SIGHT OF ME, NOR DO I EVER LOSE SIGHT OF HIM....", BHAGAVAN KRISHNA

"THE CIRCLE"

I HAD A VISION DURING YESTERDAY'S SHOWER,
THAT SIMPLIFIED EVERYTHING FOR ME,
IT HAD TO DO WITH GOD'S UNIVERSAL POWER,
AND ITS RELATIONSHIP TO ALL I SEE

I PICTURED A CIRCLE, AND CALLED IT GOD,
SO FAR, NOTHING TOO PROFOUND,
BUT, INSIDE THE CIRCLE WAS A TINY DOT,
WHICH REPRESENTED ALL THINGS AROUND

AT ONCE, I SAW THE WISDOM HERE,
AS USUAL, IT'S SO EASY TO GET,
IT PUT EVERYTHING IN PERSPECTIVE CLEAR,
FLASHING: "CAN YOU SEE NOW? WE INTERCONNECT!"

THE PEOPLE I MEET AND THE NATURE I LOVE,
ARE NOT SOME FIXTURES OR FANCY PROPS,
WE FIT TOGETHER, LIKE A HAND AND GLOVE,
COMPLETING GOD'S WORK, AND MAKING IT TOPS!

THIS SYMBOL MAKES IT SO EASY FOR ME,
ESPECIALLY WHEN I LOOK TO POINT THE FINGER,
REMINDING THAT IT'S ALSO ME I SEE,
AND SAYING: "COME MY SON, NO LONGER LINGER"

SINCE I STARTED MY PATH, I'VE HEARD MANY NAMES
USED TO DESCRIBE THE FATHER TO HIS KIDS,
AND WHILE I KNOW THAT THEY ALL MEAN THE SAME,
I CAN FINALLY RELATE TO: "ALL THAT IS"

7-21-1988

"...IF YOU SEE YOURSELF IN OTHERS, THEN WHOM CAN YOU HARM?....", HIS HOLINESS THE DALAI LAMA

"BROTHERHOOD"

I KEEP ENVISIONING WHAT'S GONNA BE,
WHEN ALL SOULS HERE BEGIN TO SEE,
AND TAKE THE TIME TO UNDERSTAND,
WE'RE ALL A PART OF THE BROTHERHOOD OF MAN

THIS ISN'T SIMPLY A FLOWERY PHRASE,
DESIGNED TO HELP US CHANGE OUR WAYS,
I HONESTLY FEEL IT IS THE TRUTH,
THE AWARENESS OF WHICH IS STILL IN ITS YOUTH

I TRY TO SEE ALL IN A DIFFERENT LIGHT,
AND IF I SOMETIMES HAVE A FIGHT,
TO LOOK AT IT WITH GOD-LIKE EYES,
AND SEEK MY BROTHER TO RECOGNIZE

FOR, BY NOW, I'VE LEARNED ONE LESSON WELL,
THAT THE BODY I SEE IS MERELY A SHELL,
THAT HOUSES GOD'S BRIGHT, INFINITE STAR,
THE TRUE CREATION OF WHO WE ARE

I MUST STRIVE TO KEEP THIS FACT IN MIND,
AND NOT BE FOOLED BY THE FAULTS I FIND,
SINCE THOSE FAULTS, IN TRUTH, BELONG TO ME,
AND MY BROTHER'S ONLY HELPING ME SEE

WE ARE AS GOD CREATED US ALL,
WHICH IS ONLY OBSCURED BECAUSE OF "THE FALL",
OUR ESSENCE IS SIMPLY JOY AND PEACE,
WITH A LOVE WITHIN THAT'LL NEVER CEASE

7-26-1988

TINKER TOYS ARE OKAY FOR BABIES……BUT MASTERS IN RECLAMATION?…….

"TRADES"

AS WE MAKE OUR WAY ALONG THE PATH,
EXPERIENCING ALL WE NEED TO GROW,
A CURIOUS THING SEEMS TO OCCUR,
SO SUBTLY, THAT WE HARDLY KNOW

IN OUR YOUNGER YEARS WE SEEMED TO PRIZE
THOSE THINGS THAT APPEAL TO EVERYONE,
BE IT PUPPY LOVE, OR RAUCOUS PARTIES,
WE PLACED GREAT STOCK IN HAVING FUN

AS WE GREW OLDER, WE TRADED THESE,
FOR THINGS THAT SEEMED SOMEWHAT SEDATE,
WE FINISHED SCHOOL, AND PURSUED A JOB,
AND RAISED THE KIDS WITH OUR CHOSEN MATE

DURING THOSE YEARS, WE BALANCED THE LOAD,
BY SPENDING SPARE TIME IN RECREATION,
IT DIDN'T MATTER WHAT FORM IT TOOK,
BE IT SPORTS, OR BOOKS, OR A NICE VACATION

THEN, QUIETLY, A WONDROUS CHANGE OCCURRED,
THE THINGS WE ONCE HELD DEAR SEEMED PALE,
YET AGAIN, WE MADE ANOTHER TRADE,
THIS TIME, WE CHOSE TO LIFT "THE VEIL"

OUR YEARS ON EARTH HAVE LED TO THIS:
WHEN THE TRUTH ABOUT BOTH LOVE AND FEAR,
IS PRESENTED FOR OUR FINAL CHOICE,
AND THE PURPOSE OF THE TRADES IS CRYSTAL CLEAR

7-27-1988

IF YOU EVER WANT TO EXPAND YOUR MIND, AND ESCAPE YOUR LIMITED WORLD, GO VISIT THE GRAND CANYON, GOD'S 100'S OF MILLIONS YEAR OLD WORK IN PROGRESS, AND EXPERIENCE THE TINY TIP OF THE ICEBERG OF ETERNITY.....GOD'S GIFT TO EVERY CREATED SOUL

"TOWARDS CLEAR PERCEPTION"

WHILE TAKING A HIKE, THIS MORNING EARL',
I GOT TO SEE A VIEW OF THE WORLD,
THAT'S USUALLY RESERVED FOR MY BROTHERS, THE BIRDS,
AND GIVES A BROAD PICTURE OF OUR MOTHER EARTH

AS I STOOD ATOP THE GENTLE HILL,
AND GAZED AT THE VILLAGE, SLEEPING STILL,
BENEATH WERE THE PARTS THAT COMPRISED THE TOWN,
BY SHIFTING MY EYES, I COULD SEE ALL AROUND

WHILE CONTEMPLATING THE SIGHT BELOW,
A MORNING BREEZE BEGAN TO BLOW,
THIS WAS MY SIGNAL TO PAY CLOSE HEED,
AND HEAR GOD'S MESSAGE, CARRIED BY HER SWIFT STEED

MOMENTS LATER, A THOUGHT ENTERED MY MIND,
WHICH HELPED ME TO LEAVE MY SMALL WORLD BEHIND,
A WORLD EXISTING IN A TINY BOX,
WHICH MY FRIGHTENED ego *KEEPS TRYING TO LOCK*

IT SAID: " EVERYTHING SEEMS SO VERY SMALL,
WHEN PEERED FROM HIGH ABOVE THE WALLS,
THAT FORM THE PRISON OF YOUR ego self,
WHICH, INCIDENTALLY, IS YOUR PERSONAL HELL

REMEMBER THIS VISION, AND YOU HAVE THE KEY,
THAT OFFERS YOU FREEDOM FOR ETERNITY,
THIS WORLD IS ONLY A TINY PART,
OF THE KINGDOM OF GOD WITHIN YOUR HEART!"

7-30-1988

BELOVED MASTER JESUS KNEW THE TRUTH ABOUT WHO AND WHAT HE WAS AND WHO WE ARE…. THE GREATEST WORDS HE GAVE TO HUMANITY WERE: "OUR FATHER"

"PERCEPTION VERSUS KNOWLEDGE"

I'M LEARNING THERE'S AN UNDERSTANDING,
THAT EACH OF US MUST GAIN,
BEFORE WE TRULY KNOW OUR "SELVES"
AND THE KNOWLEDGE WE CONTAIN

WE'VE WRITTEN MANY TIMES BEFORE,
SINCE MY PATH'S EARLY INCEPTION,
THAT EVERYTHING WE THINK AND FEEL
IS BASED ON OUR PERCEPTION

PERCEPTION'S THE FALSE AWARENESS
THAT WE GAIN THROUGH OUR FIVE SENSES,
WHILE KNOWLEDGE IS THE CERTAINTY
WHICH COMES FROM KNOWING "WHAT IS"

IF YOU STOOD OUTSIDE, ON A CLOUDY DAY,
CONVERSING WITH SOMEONE,
YOU'D PROBABLY SAY, WITH CERTAINTY,
THAT, ABOVE THOSE CLOUDS, SHINES THE SUN

IF THEY NEVER KNEW A SUNNY DAY,
THEY'D BELIEVE JUST WHAT THEY SAW,
UNLESS THEY HAD GREAT FAITH IN YOU,
THEY'D PERCEIVE THE SUN BELONGED TO LORE

PERCEPTIONS CAN NEVER SHOW THE TRUTH,
SINCE THEY RELY ON WHAT WE SEE,
BUT, IF CLEAR, THEY PROVIDE A STEPPING STONE
TO GOD'S KNOWLEDGE AND ITS CERTAINTY

8-04-1988

TWO CLASSES IN MOTHER EARTH'S SCHOOL OF POSSIBILITIES, ALTHOUGH I BELIEVE THAT SCHOOL IS COMING TO AN END ON THIS PLANET

"TRANSFIGURATION VERSUS ANNIHILATION"*

TODAY MARKS THE ANNIVERSARY,
OF TWO SPECIAL EVENTS IN MAN'S HISTORY,
WHICH MANIFESTED, FOR ALL TO SEE,
TWO OPTIONS FOR HOW WE MAY CHOOSE TO BE

THE FIRST ONE HAPPENED AWHILE BACK,
AND STARTED WITH A MORNING ATTACK,
ON A CITY THAT BEGAN JUST ANOTHER DAY,
AND ENDED IT BY BEING DESTROYED A NEW WAY

THROUGH A COMBINATION OF MAN'S TECHNOLOGY,
AND THE AWESOME POWER OF CREATIVITY,
AFTER WAKING TO OUR FATHER'S MORNING SUN,
THE PEOPLE WERE SNUFFED BY WHAT MAN HAD DONE

THE SECOND EVENT REALLY HAPPENED FIRST,
SINCE IT TOOK PLACE LONG BEFORE THE WORST,
DURING THE TIME CHRIST WALKED THE EARTH,
TEACHING HIS BROTHERS ABOUT THEIR TRUE WORTH

HE TOOK THREE DISCIPLES ATOP A MOUNTAIN CLEAR,
AND TOLD THEM THERE WAS NO NEED FOR FEAR,
AS HE SHOWED TO THEM HIS BODY OF LIGHT,
AND DEMONSTRATED OUR FATHER'S AMAZING MIGHT

BOTH EVENTS WERE DESIGNED TO TEACH,
THAT EITHER OF THEM WAS WITHIN MAN'S REACH,
THE ONE COULD BE CALLED UPON TO DESTROY,
WHILE THE OTHER GAVE PROMISE OF ETERNAL JOY

**In the Catholic tradition, August 6 is the feast of The Transfiguration of Jesus...*

8-06-1988

MIKEY CHRISTIE SAYS: "...TIME IS VERY GENTLE TO THOSE WHO FOLLOW THEIR HEARTS....UNCONDITIONALLY..."

"8-8-88"

THIS IS A VERY SPECIAL DAY,
FOR THOSE TRAVELLING THROUGH TIME AND SPACE,
IT ONLY OCCURS EVERY ELEVEN YEARS,
WHICH, TO US, IS A REAL SNAIL'S PACE

IT'S WHEN THE DAY, THE MONTH AND YEAR
ALL SHARE THE VERY SAME NUMBER,
IF WE LOOKED AT THE LAST TIME THIS OCCURRED,
WE'D SURELY BE FILLED WITH WONDER

FOR, IT DIDN'T SEEM THAT LONG AGO,
AS I LOOK BACK ON IT TODAY,
AND YET, SO MUCH HAS TAKEN PLACE,
THAT HELPED ME ON MY "WAY"

'CAUSE THIS IS WHY WE WERE GIVEN TIME,
I BELIEVE THIS TO BE SO,
IT'S MEANT TO HELP US LEARN THE LESSONS,
WE EACH NEED IN ORDER TO GROW

YES, I FEEL THAT TIME EXISTS FOR US,
ONLY HERE ON MOTHER EARTH,
SINCE HEAVEN HAS NO NEED FOR IT,
BEING AWARE OF ITS TRUE WORTH

THERE'LL COME A TIME EACH ONE OF US,
RECOGNIZES THEIR SHINING STAR,
IT DOESN'T MATTER HOW LONG IT TAKES,
FOR, GOD KNOWS WHO WE ARE

8-08-1988

"A COURSE IN MIRACLES" STATES: "….I AM NOT A BODY, I AM FREE, I AM AS GOD CREATED ME….". THE MOVIES "COCOON" AND "STARMAN" GIVE US A NICE PICTURE OF THE CONCEPT

"PURIFICATION II"

THERE'S ANOTHER THING TO BE RELEASED,
ON MY JOURNEY HOME TO GOD'S INFINITE PEACE,
THAT HAS TO DO WITH THIS BODY I SEE,
AND THE MIS-BELIEF THAT IT'S REALLY ME

I'VE NEVER BEEN AFRAID MY TRUTH TO TELL,
I BELIEVE OUR BODIES ARE SIMPLY SHELLS,
THAT ARE HOMES FOR GOD'S CREATIONS TRUE,
IN SHORT, THAT MEANS BOTH ME AND YOU

JUST AS MY CAR IS MERELY THE MEANS,
FOR ME TO GO FROM A TO B,
THE SAME CAN BE SAID OF THIS VEHICLE,
THAT ALLOWS ME TO WALK, WHILE DOING GOD'S WILL

THERE'S A SECOND ILLUSTRATION FOR ME,
I THINK OF PEOPLE WHO CANNOT SEE,
THE THINGS PERCEIVED THROUGH OUR PHYSICAL EYES,
BECAUSE THEY ARE, AS WE TERM, BLIND

BEING SUCH, THEY CAN ONLY SEE YOU,
BY WHAT YOU SAY AND WHAT YOU DO,
IT MATTERS NOT, BE YOU YOUNG OR OLD,
FOR, THESE "SIGHTLESS" ONES CAN SEE YOUR SOUL

THESE VERY SIMPLE ANALOGIES,
ARE ALL I NEED TO HELP ME SEE,
WE ARE THE PERFECTION THAT GOD CREATED,
ONCE THE BODY HAS BEEN NEGATED

8-13-1988

IN THE MOVIE, "THE LAST TEMPTATION OF CHRIST", JESUS ASKS HIS BEST FRIEND, JUDAS, TO BETRAY HIM. JUDAS PROTESTS THAT HE COULD NEVER DO SUCH A THING TO A FRIEND, TO WHICH JESUS REPLIES: "...THAT'S WHY YOU HAVE THE HARDER JOB..."

"PERFECT SAFETY"

I'M GOING TO OFFER ANOTHER VIEW,
OF AN EVENT THAT HAPPENED AWHILE BACK,
IN ORDER TO SHOW BOTH ME AND YOU,
THAT WE CAN NEVER, REALLY, BE ATTACKED

WE'VE ALL HEARD OF CHRIST'S AGONY,
AND THE PART OF IT PLAYED BY JUDAS,
HE WAS THE DISCIPLE WHO, FOR A FEE,
BETRAYED HIS MASTER WITH A KISS

BECAUSE OF THAT, HE HUNG HIMSELF,
WHO KNOWS WHAT WAS TRULY IN HIS MIND,
PERHAPS HE THOUGHT HE'D GO TO HELL,
OR MAYBE, IT WAS PARADISE THAT HE'D FIND

FOR, WHAT IF THE MASTER REQUESTED HIM,
BECAUSE HE WAS HIS CLOSEST FRIEND,
TO LET THE WORLD THINK ***he*** *HAD SINNED,*
BY HELPING TO LEAD HIM TO HIS END

I BELIEVE CHRIST CHOSE TO BE CRUCIFIED,
TO TEACH THE WORLD A NEEDED LESSON,
TO LET THEM THINK THAT HE HAD "DIED",
BECAUSE OF ALL THEIR ACTS OF AGGRESSION

BUT, JESUS KNEW WHO HE, IN FACT, WAS,
THAT HE, LIKE US, WAS OF GOD A SON,
AND SO, HE TAUGHT US WE WERE LOVE,
BY MEANS OF HIS "DEATH" AND RESURRECTION

8-20-1988

I BELIEVE WE WERE SENT HERE AGES AGO TO DEMONSTRATE OUR LOVE/WISDOM NATURE TO OUR NEIGHBORS IN THE COSMOS, AND TO BE CARETAKERS OF THIS MAGNIFICENT ENTITY WE CALL MOTHER EARTH… I ALSO BELIEVE WE CAN STILL TURN THINGS AROUND

"CARETAKERS"

AS I WATCHED THE MOON SMILING DOWN ON ME,
WITH ALL THE STARS WINKING KNOWINGLY,
I ASKED MY SELF, "WHO COULD EVER DOUBT
THERE'S A POWER BEHIND ALL CREATION?"

I SOMETIMES SENSE MY POINT OF ORIGIN,
IS THERE AMONGST THOSE BRILLIANT STARS,
AND I FEEL THAT I'M JUST VISITING HERE,
BUT I'M NOT QUITE SURE JUST WHY

I HEAR THE NEWS, AND I READ IT TOO,
AND THE IMAGES SEEM SAD AND HOPELESS,
I SEE BROTHER ATTACKING BROTHER AT WILL,
AND NO REGARD FOR THE LIFE THAT'S AROUND US

BUT, WHILE I STOOD GAZING AT MY ORIGINAL HOME,
THE VOICE WITHIN SOFTLY SPOKE,
REMINDING ME THAT I CAME LONG AGO,
TO COMPLETE AN IMPORTANT ROLE

IT SAID I ARRIVED, LIKE EVERYONE ELSE,
TO CARE FOR ALL LIFE ON THE PLANET,
BE IT FISH OR FOWL, OR PLANT OR ROCK,
I WAS TO LOVE ALL, AS I DO MY PARENT

YET, MY JOB HAD AN EXTRA CLAUSE, YOU SEE,
THIS WAS AT MY SOUL'S REQUEST,
I WAS TO AWAKEN SOME OF MY SLEEPING BROTHERS AND SISTERS
AND SHARE OUR FATHER'S MESSAGE

8-22-1988

DIANA, BELOVED MASTER MERLIN'S "MOUTHPIECE", LIKED TO REFER TO THOSE CHILLS WE GET WHEN SOMETHING RESONATES IN OUR BEING, AS..."ANGEL FLESH"

"SPIRITUAL HARVEST"

AS I MOVE CLOSER TO BECOMING WHOLE,
BY MANIFESTING MY ETERNAL SOUL,
I'M NOTICING SOME PLEASANT ATTRIBUTES,
WHICH ARE ALSO KNOWN AS SPIRITUAL FRUITS

I SEEM TO BE FEELING A GREATER LOVE,
FOR ALL CREATED BY THE POWER ABOVE,
BE IT BROTHER OR A VERDANT POD,
I ALWAYS SENSE THE PRESENCE OF GOD

THE MORE I WAKE AND BECOME AWARE,
THERE ISN'T EVER A SINGLE CARE,
TO CAUSE IN ME CONFLICT OR FUSS,
BECAUSE MY SELF'S GUIDANCE I DO TRUST

GIVING TO OTHERS BRINGS GREAT JOY,
'CAUSE I DON'T ACKNOWLEDGE THE ego's PLOY,
THAT TRIES TO MAKE ME THINK I LOSE,
WHEN I SHARE OR GIVE TO WHOM I CHOOSE

I ALSO FIND THAT DOING GOD'S WILL,
CAUSES MY BODY TO FEEL A CHILL,
WHETHER SPEAKING, OR WRITING, OR SHARING MY TIME,
I'M GRATEFUL FOR THIS COSMIC SIGN

EACH CYCLE OF THE DAY AND NIGHT,
DRAWS ME NEARER TO GOD'S NURTURING LIGHT,
THIS MAN NO LONGER WEEPS OR WAILS,
FOR, THE TIME'S AT HAND TO LIFT THE VEIL

9-03-1988

THIS POEM WAS WRITTEN JUST AFTER TALKING WITH A SWEET, RETIRED COLLEGE PROFESSOR WHOM I FIRST SAW PLAY ETHEL THAYER IN A LOCAL PRODUCTION OF "ON GOLDEN POND", AND WHOM I LATER MET AT A "BEYOND WAR" MEETING. HER NAME WAS ELLY...A TRUE CO-HEART

"SIMPLICITY"

I HAD A PLEASANT CHAT WITH A FRIEND TODAY,
SHARING IDEAS THAT HELPED EACH OF US SEE,
WE DISCUSSED MANY THINGS, BUT WHAT PROMPTED THIS VERSE,
WAS OUR MUTUAL WISH FOR SIMPLICITY

SO, I STARTED TO DREAM, AND PICTURED A HOME,
ON A BLUFF OVERLOOKING THE DEEP, BLUE SEA,
WITH PLENTY OF SPACE FOR MILES AROUND,
AND BEHIND ME, A STAND OF FRAGRANT PINE TREES

BUT WHAT WOULD I DO, I ASKED MY SELF,
TO LIVE, AND TO SERVE MY BROTHERS AS WELL,
UNLIKE MY ABODE, NO PICTURES APPEARED,
SO I LISTENED FOR THE LESSON, MY TEACHER WOULD TELL

HE SAID: "FIRST OF ALL, REMEMBER, YOU TRUST
THAT ALL IN YOUR LIFE'S FOR A DEFINITE REASON,
CONTINUE TO STAY WHERE YOU ARE, RIGHT NOW,
AND KNOW THAT YOU'LL BLOOM WHEN IT IS YOUR SEASON"

SHE NEXT REMINDED ME OF WHAT I SEEK:
TO KNOW MY "SELF", AND MY BROTHERS TOO,
WHILE LEARNING TO ENDURE THE THINGS OF THE WORLD,
NO MATTER THE TESTS IT PUTS ME THROUGH

AND FINALLY, GOD POINTED TO ALL OF THE GIFTS,
THAT I ENJOY BOTH NIGHT AND DAY,
I SUDDENLY FELT TRUTH WASH OVER ME,
AND WAS HAPPY, AGAIN, TO CONTINUE MY WAY

9-13-1988

HERE IS AN EXCERPT OF A DESCRIPTION BELOVED MASTER MERLIN GAVE ON BEING: "…THE BEING IS…THE BEING ALWAYS SPEAKS THE TRUTH…THE BEING ALWAYS SPEAKS WITH LOVE…THE BEING HAS COURAGE…THE BEING CANNOT FEAR ATTACK, OR JUDGMENT OR LACK OF APPROVAL…"

"BEING"

THESE DAYS I'M GROWING MORE AWARE,
AS I LEARN TO DISCERN MOST EVERYTHING,
AND SEPARATE WHAT APPEARS TO BE THERE,
FROM WHAT, INDEED, HAS REAL "BE"- ING

I'VE LONG ACCEPTED IN MY HEART,
THAT WHAT IS REAL, IS ETERNAL TOO,
BUT OFTIMES I GET SO RAPT IN MY "PART",
THAT I FREQUENTLY FORGET WHAT I'M HERE TO DO

THESE LITTLE PLAYS THAT WE ACT OUT,
ARE, TO ME, THE SAME AS DREAMS,
I SAY THIS NOW, WHILE NOT RUNNING ABOUT,
REACTING TO ALL THAT SO REAL SEEMS

BUT, I FEEL ALL THINGS ARE A TEMPORAL VIEW,
IF THEY CAN BE SEEN WITH MY NAKED EYES,
SINCE I'VE SAID WHAT'S REAL MUST BE FOREVER TRUE,
THEN, I'M TRYING TO EXIST IN A WORLD OF LIES

I MUST STRIVE TO LOOK HARD AT THE THINGS I SEE,
BY FILTERING THROUGH ONLY DIVINE, PURE LOVE,
IGNORING THE PART THAT CAN NEVER "BE",
AND RELATING TO ALL THAT'S LIKE ABOVE

I HAVE TWO OPTIONS IN TIME AND SPACE,
THROUGH THE GRACE OF OUR FATHER, THE CHOICE IS FREE,
I CAN EITHER EXIST AS A MEMBER OF THIS RACE,
OR AWAKEN TO WHO GOD KNOWS ME TO "BE"

9-22-1988

"...LOVE IS REAL...REAL IS LOVE...LOVE IS WANTING TO BE LOVED...LOVE IS KNOWING WE CAN BE...", EXCERPTS FROM JOHN LENNON'S SONG "LOVE"

"WHAT REALLY MATTERS"

HOW OFTEN HAVE I ALLOWED MYSELF,
TO GET CAUGHT UP IN THE DAILY GRIND,
ACTING LIKE A CAT ON A HOT, TIN ROOF,
UNTIL I REMEMBER: IT DOESN'T MATTER

ego's LIVE LIKE CLASHING CYMBALS,
BECAUSE THEY WANT TO BE SEPARATE,
I'VE DONE THAT MANY TIME BEFORE,
BUT, NOW I KNOW: IT DOESN'T MATTER

I'D FREQUENTLY FRET ABOUT WHAT MIGHT HAPPEN,
IF MY JOB SHOULD SUDDENLY BE NO MORE,
GETTING INVOLVED IN THE SPECULATIONS,
'TIL I HEARD THE ANSWER: IT DOESN'T MATTER

THE SEASONS COME, AND THE SEASONS GO,
THE GRAND CANYON WAS JUST A MIGHTY RIVER,
I'M LEARNING EVERYTHING HERE IS TEMPORARY,
AND BECAUSE OF THAT: IT DOESN'T MATTER

ON EARTH, THERE SEEMS TO BE A CHOICE,
'TWEEN LIVING IN TIME OR IN ETERNITY,
ONCE WE CHOOSE TO "BE" ETERNAL,
THEN, ABOUT TIME WE SAY: IT DOESN'T MATTER

I BELIEVE OUR FATHER CREATED US LIKE HIM,
FOREVER PERFECT, AND FILLED WITH LOVE,
THUS, THERE'S ONLY ONE THING THAT'S REAL:
GOD'S INFINITE LOVE; AHH, THAT'S ALL THAT MATTERS

10-06-1988

"...TWO ROADS DIVERGED IN A YELLOW WOOD, AND SORRY I COULD NOT TRAVEL BOTH, AND BE ONE TRAVELER, LONG I STOOD AND LOOKED DOWN ONE, UNTIL IT BENT IN THE UNDERGROWTH...", FROM ROBERT FROST'S "THE ROAD NOT TAKEN"...THERE ARE SO MANY ROADS TO TAKE

"THE ROAD NOW TAKEN"

I'M GLEANING A THEME FROM ROBERT FROST,
SO I CAN SING OF A "LITTLE BOY LOST",
WHO LEARNED TO CONQUER A DEEP, DARK FEAR,
BY TRUSTING HIS TRUE SELF WAS ALWAYS NEAR

THE SUBJECT SOUL SPENT MOST OF HIS LIFE,
SHARING HIS TIME WITH A LOVELY WIFE,
HAVING GOTTEN MARRIED WHILE IN HIS TEENS,
HE HAD NO IDEA WHAT TRUE FREEDOM MEANS

THEY RAISED THREE CHILDREN AS BEST THEY KNEW,
AND LEARNED OF LIFE AS THE BABIES GREW,
TOGETHER, THEY COULD DO 'MOST ANYTHING,
THEY WERE, INDEED, AN EXCELLENT TEAM

BUT, IN HIS HEART, THE BOY HAD A DREAM,
THAT THINGS DIDN'T HAVE TO BE AS THEY SEEMED,
BECAUSE OF THIS, HE ALWAYS KNEW,
THAT HE WAS SIMPLY JUST PASSING THROUGH

AND THEN, ONE DAY, HE HEARD THE CALL,
ANSWERING IT BY CHANGING ALL,
OF THE BELIEFS HE HELD 'TIL THEN,
STARTING WITH: WANTING TO SERVE ALL MEN

TO DO THIS AND TRULY LEARN TO SEE,
HE FELT HE HAD TO BE TOTALLY FREE,
TO CHANGE DIRECTIONS WHEN HE NEEDED TO,
AND TRUST THAT GOD WOULD HELP HIM THROUGH

10-15-1988

A WEED HAS BEEN DESCRIBED AS AN UNWELCOME PLANT IN MOST GARDENS...DANDELIONS AND THISTLES, WITH THEIR BRIGHT YELLOW AND PURPLE FLOWERS, ARE BEAUTIFUL, IN THEIR OWN WAY. HANNIBAL LECTER, WAS A PSYCHOPATH, BUT ALSO A CHARMING HOST...THIS WORLD OF DUALITY...

"GARDENS"

I'M FINDING IN EACH AND EVERY DAY,
A NEW DISCOVERY TO LIGHT MY WAY,
THIS LATEST ONE APPEALS TO ME,
FOR, IT TEACHES WITH THINGS THAT I CAN SEE

IT PICTURES A GARDEN IN EACH OF OUR MINDS,
WITH COLORFUL FLOWERS OF EVERY KIND,
AMIDST THE BLOSSOMS AND ALL OF THEIR SEEDS,
ARE SOME UGLY AND STRANGLING, NASTY WEEDS

THE FLOWERS, OF COURSE, ARE SYMBOLS OF LOVE,
DEPICTING ALL THINGS THAT STEM FROM ABOVE,
WHILE THE WEEDS ARE THERE IN ORDER TO SHOW,
THOSE PARTS OF US STILL ANCHORED BELOW

LOVE, AND PEACE, AND JOY, AND TRUTH,
ARE ROSES AND VIOLETS WITH ETERNAL YOUTH,
WHILE FEAR, AND ANGER, AND ANXIETY,
ARE HARBINGERS OF DEATH BROUGHT ON BY DIS-EASE

I'M STRIVING ALL TIMES IN MY GARDEN TO GROW,
ALL OF THE FLOWERS THAT WILL TEACH ME TO "KNOW",
SO, WHEN DEALING WITH ANOTHER WHO HELPS ME TO SEE,
I SHARE A SEED FROM THEIR FLOWERS, AND IGNORE THE WEEDS

I WANT MY GARDEN TO BE THE VERY BEST,
TO SHOW OUR FATHER I'VE PASSED ALL THE TESTS,
AND BE AN EXAMPLE OF CHRIST'S WORDS LONG AGO:
"...YOU REAP EXACTLY WHAT YOU SOW..."

11-07-1988

THIS WAS THE LAST POEM I WAS TO WRITE IN THIS FORMAT…IT LED TO A NEW STYLE OF POETRY AND SOME OTHER VERY INTERESTING ESSAYS

"THE LAMPLIGHTER"

I HAVEN'T WRITTEN FOR QUITE AWHILE,
THERE SIMPLY WASN'T THAT OLD DESIRE,
BUT, TODAY'S IDEA CAUSED A GREAT BIG SMILE,
IGNITING THE SPARK OF GOD'S GOLDEN FIRE

CHRIST SAID HE WAS THE LIGHT OF THE WORLD,
THAT HE WAS THE TRUTH FOR YOU AND ME,
AS MY LIFE'S TAPESTRY CONTINUES TO UNFURL,
IT'S OBVIOUS WHAT I'M STRIVING TO BE

I, AS YOU, AM A CHILD OF GOD,
CREATED LIKE HIM, A BEING OF LIGHT,
FOR MOST OF US, THAT ACCEPTANCE IS HARD,
'CAUSE WE'VE SPENT OUR LIVES CONSUMED WITH FRIGHT

THAT FEAR AROSE FOR DENYING THE TRUTH,
GUILT-RIDDEN, WE BELIEVED WE HAD TO DIE,
FOR SPURNING OUR FATHER, LIKE SPOILED YOUTHS,
WE LOWERED THE VEIL, AND LIVED A LIE

BUT, WHAT I'M REMEMBERING FEELS TRUE TO ME,
THAT GOD NEVER LEFT US, SHE LOVES US SO,
I TOO, AM A LIGHT THAT'S LEARNING TO SEE,
AND I WANT TO SHARE THAT WITH ALL OF YOU

WHEN I'M FULLY AWAKE, MY LIGHT WILL GLOW,
AND MY FLAME WILL BE EASY FOR ALL TO FIND,
FOR THOSE WHO'VE WEARIED OF CRINGING BELOW,
I'LL LIGHT THE LAMP THAT'S IN THEIR MIND

4-06-1989

PART III

THE "LAMPLIGHTER" WRITINGS

10-25-1989

Thru

9-10-2000

"OUR FATHER"

P *ATIENCE WHEN WE TEND TO DOUBT,*
E *NLIGHTENMENT'S WHAT IT'S ALL ABOUT,*
A *CCEPTING THE THINGS WE CANNOT CHANGE,*
C *HANGING THE ONES THAT SEEM SO STRANGE,*
E *VERY OCCURRENCE IS MEANT TO TEACH,*

A *ND HELP EACH SOUL ITS GOAL TO REACH,*
N *OTHING WE SEE IS THE TOTAL TRUTH,*
D *ESPITE THE THINGS WE'VE LEARNED SINCE YOUTH,*

L *OVE IS WHO CREATED US ALL,*
O *VER AND OVER, HE SENDS THE CALL,*
V *OWING TO WELCOME EACH ONE OF US HOME,*
E *TERNALLY DWELLING WITH HIM, AS ONE,*

A *LL IT TAKES FOR A LASTING SMILE:*
N *EVER DENY YOU ARE HIS CHILD,*
D *IFFERENCES ARE MERELY GRAND ILLUSIONS,*

T *ESTING THE STRENGTH OF OUR TRUST IN UNION,*
R *EBELLION IS OUR ego's VAIN ATTEMPT AT*
U *NDOING THE WILL THAT'S HEAVEN SENT,*
T *OGETHER, WE'LL COMPLETE OUR FATHER'S PLAN,*
H *APPILY WALKING HAND IN HAND*

10-25-1989

"A CHILD'S PRAYER"

Our Father, Who dwells deep within us,

How comforting is Your Name.

Remembrance of You reveals Your eternal gifts

Of Love to each of us,

As it also reminds us that Your Will is ours,

There being no other.

Each day, you nourish our Souls,

As well as our bodies,

While overlooking our mistakes, and asking us

To do the same for our brothers,

Because You know we are just sleeping.

You remind us that You are All in All,

And everything that is not Love, isn't True.

Through Your Voice in our Hearts,

You are guiding us Home, back to Your Loving Arms,

Where we have always been, and always will be,

Together with all of Your Glorious Creation,

Now and Forever.......Amen

10-28-1989

HOW "A CHILD'S PRAYER" CAME ABOUT

I began my "AWAKENING" nearly 3 years ago, on my fortieth birthday, which was November 25, 1986. For the next 2 years, I wrote down my feelings and new understandings in the form of ditties, poems and even letters to the local newspaper. I would also use my poetry as a means of sharing a gift of Love with various individuals in my life.

On December 31, 1988, I wrote my last poem, which was a gift of Love to my Aunt Frances, and created Issue 2 of "BABYSTEPS", which is a book of some of my poetry. With the exception of a poem titled "THE LAMPLIGHTER", which I wrote back in April, there had been no inspiration to write anything at all this year. Then, one day in October, while I was at work, I began to write the words PEACE AND LOVE AND TRUTH vertically, and next thing I knew, "OUR FATHER" was created, along with a completely different style of writing poetry, for me.

A few days later, at 2:00 AM on the morning of October 28, 1989, I AWAKENED suddenly, thinking of the "OUR FATHER" and how I would express it to the world with my current understanding of our relationship to God. So, I'd like to share those thoughts with you because, as with everything I've been doing these past 3 years, it feels right.

I'll look at each phrase of "A CHILD'S PRAYER", and put the original words that Jesus gave us, during THE SERMON ON THE MOUNT, alongside it. These are my understandings, as I perceive them NOW, and they are not meant to attack or weaken anyone's beliefs. If they strike a chord within your Soul, so be it. If not, that's OK, too. Whatever we believe, we are all, indeed, Children of God, or some Force greater than we, because we did not create ourselves. In that Light, we are all brothers and sisters and I Love each of you for Who I believe you Truly are.

Love, Always,
Michael

11-20-1989

"A CHILD'S PRAYER"	"THE OUR FATHER"
Our Father	*Our Father*

These are perhaps the 2 most beautiful words ever given to humanity. With them, Jesus acknowledged that God was "OUR FATHER" and that He, Jesus, was our brother (how often does Jesus address those listening as "my brethren" or brothers?). Being our Father, God Loves us with an intensity that is inconceivable in this world. He cares for and watches over us and only wants us to be Happy, and to REMEMBER that we are all His Children.

Who dwells deep within us	*Who art in Heaven*

Jesus said that the Kingdom of Heaven is within each one of us, and that we are temples of God. There is, deep within our Beings, a "Star Seed" that contains all the attributes of our Father and is actually an extension of Him. Jesus understood this when He said: "I and my Father are ONE".

How comforting is Your Name	*Hallowed be Thy Name*

Whenever we are tempted to forget that God is always with us, because we are too caught up in the world we see and fall prey to feelings of loneliness, despair, depression, anxiety, scarcity, sorrow, etc., all we need do is think of "HIM" and allow His Peace to surround us. Once again, we will be safe in His Arms.

Remembrance of You reveals Your Eternal gifts of Love to each of us	*Thy Kingdom come*

Being created in God's Image, we are Perfect and have everything we need, or ever will need, right NOW. God gave us All That He Is; Love, Wisdom, Peace, Joy, Abundance, Creativity and Eternal Life. We are like PERFECT diamonds that He created, but because we covered those diamonds of Love with the mud of fear, we have a mistaken belief about Who we really are.

As it also reminds us that Your Will is ours, there being no other	*Thy Will be done on Earth, as It is in Heaven*

With those words, Jesus tried to convey the understanding that there is only God's Will and that the idea of separation from Him leads us to believe that there is a will apart from His. Again, if The Kingdom of Heaven is within us, then It can't be apart from us. Heaven is Unity. It is only in this world that we perceive separation between each other and everything around us (rather than seeing our bodies as communication devices, we see them as fences which separate us from everyone else). When Jesus said that He was in the world (of fear), but not of it, I believe He was reminding us to always "BE" God's Loving Child despite what we see going on around us. We were to be like oil on water.

Each day, You nourish our Souls, as well as our bodies	*Give us this day our daily bread*

Jesus tried to impress His disciples with God's Love for us by pointing out how, if God even notes the falling of a tiny sparrow, how much does He care for His Beloved Children. If we are honest, we will see that we always have had food to eat and a roof over our heads. But more than that, the Spiritual nourishment we receive daily, hourly, each moment that we walk the Earth, through the Loving thoughts, words and deeds that we express, is the Eternal Food of Life (God's Law of Love states that what we say or do to another, we say or do to ourselves). Jesus once said that if a person drank water, they would thirst again, but if they drank and ate the Water and Bread of Life, they would never go thirsty or hungry. God is Love and God is Life, and when we feel separate from Him or are not Loving, then, we are dead or dying.

While overlooking our mistakes, and asking us to do the same for our brothers, because You know we are just sleeping	*And forgive us our trespasses, as we forgive those who who trespass against us*

Perhaps the greatest lesson Jesus came to teach was FORGIVENESS. As He was "dying" on the cross, He asked His Father to forgive his "murderers" because they didn't really know what they were doing. They thought they were killing Him, but Jesus showed that THERE IS NO DEATH, and that the Power of God within Him was able to revivify

His broken and lifeless body. We are like children with amnesia who think we are someone else, and God is the Loving and Patient Parent Who remembers Who His Children really are. Would anyone withhold forgiveness from a brother or sister who said or did something terrible to them while suffering from amnesia?

You remind us that You are ALL in ALL, and everything that is not Love, isn't True

And lead us not into temptation,

God is Love. God is Truth. God is Real. Therefore, Love and Truth are Real, while fear and illusions are false. This statement will even appeal to the logical mind, because the above conditions cannot both be True, since they contradict each other. If we are tempted to believe in the temporal world of fear, we need only remember God's Eternal Heaven of Love That is within us. Then, we can perceive the world through the Eyes of Love instead of fear.

Through Your Voice in our Hearts, You are guiding us Home, back to Your Loving Arms,

But deliver us from evil

Jesus said He would not leave us comfortless, but that "The Great Comforter", The Holy (Whole-I) Spirit, would always help us. The Holy Spirit is The Voice for God That is in our Hearts. Another word might be "INTUITION". The Holy Spirit will separate the True from the false, as long as there is duality in this world. We must learn to differentiate between The Voice of Love in our Hearts, and the voice of fear, or the ego, that occupies a small part of our minds. The ego's voice wants to separate God's Child and lead him to hell, or away from God, while The Holy Spirit wants to help us remember our True Identity and lead us Home.

Where we have always been, and always will BE, together with all of Your Glorious Creation,

For Thine is The Kingdom, and The Power and The Glory

We have never left our Father, nor has He left us. We are as God created us, and all the false beliefs we have about ourselves can never change that. Columbus proved that belief doesn't make something True. We are the PERFECT, sparkling diamonds that are part of the Treasure House of God. As long as even one of us has amnesia, God's Treasure House is incomplete. God can give Himself everything except our Love, that we must offer to Him. We must AWAKEN and claim our rightful place in The Kingdom. Our Father is waiting for His wayward Sons and Daughters to return Home.

Now and Forever *Forever and ever*

God always was, is NOW, and always will BE......"I AM THAT I AM". Time does not exist in Eternity, since it is infinite, but to get an understanding of Eternity in this finite world, we must always BE in the present moment, or NOW. This will allow us to escape from the past, and have no interest in the future. This also eliminates judgment, for without the past, judgment is impossible. Without judgment, the world is INNOCENT and PURE, rather than guilty and stained. Jesus used the symbol of the lamb to illustrate that we are all like INNOCENT LAMBS, for in God's Eyes, we are sinless. God creates Perfection, and to believe that we are less than that, is not humbleness, but an arrogance that serves our ego's rather than our Souls.

Amen *Amen*

This word is "The Word". It is the most Powerful Word, or Sound, in all Creation, because It is the Cause of Creation, the Cosmic Generator, if you will. For this discussion, It can mean "So Be It" or "So It Is". The ancients have always understood the Power of "The Word" and referred to It as "A-U-M", Which is also expressed as "OM". We have no idea of the Power of "The Word", unless open minded people can look at the countless galaxies in the known universe as some indication, but, Jesus knew Its Power and by closing His prayer with "The Word", knew that It was accomplished in Heaven, at the same moment It was spoken on Earth.

An observation: I find it interesting that the prayer spoken 2,000 years ago, and the one written last week, opened and closed identically, with the words "Our Father" and "Amen". Truth transcends time.

"BIRD OF PARADISE"

The ancients often referred to the Soul as "The Bird of Paradise" That was encased within the seeming limitations of the flesh and blood of our bodies. Actually, as Jesus demonstrated, the only limitation on this Earth is the fear that is expressed by our ego's, or the part of our minds that believes it is separate from God. We are Love, created by Love, and nothing will ever change that fact. Once we remember WHOM WE ARE ONE with, all the Power, Love, Wisdom, Joy and Abundance of Heaven will be ours again.

I was inspired to write this little dissertation and accompanying poem because of a gift that one of my co-workers received today. It was a beautiful floral arrangement that included two spectacular Bird of Paradise flowers, one of my very favorite flora.

I started my journey Home on 11-25-1986, nearly 3 years ago, and it appears that this poem will close out the third year. I also feel it is fitting that I'm penning these words on Thanksgiving eve. So, in that Light, God bless you all, and have a great Thanksgiving, every day of your Life!

B *OTTLED UP WITHIN FLESH AND BONE,*
I *TS EARTHLY GOAL IS TO FIND THE WAY HOME,*
R *ATHER THAN STRUGGLE WITH THE WORLD THAT IT SEES, ITS ONLY*
D *ESIRE IS TO FLY AND BE FREE*

O *NCE THE CAGE HAS BEEN RECOGNIZED, THE*
F *ATHER REJOICES AT HIS CHILD'S OPENING EYES*

P *ART OF THE JOURNEY BACK HOME TO HIM, IS*
A *NSWERING THE CALL OF HIS VOICE WITHIN*
R *EMEMBRANCE OF WHO EACH ONE OF US IS,*
A *LLOWS OUR FATHER TO RESTORE HIS GIFTS*
D *OUBT NO LONGER EXISTS IN THE MIND,*
I *NTUITION GUARANTEES OUR TRUE SELF WE'LL FIND*
S *O, WELCOME THE FLAPS OF THE WINGS OF YOUR SOUL,*
E *ARTHBOUND NO LONGER, IT'S, ONCE AGAIN, WHOLE*

11-22-1989

"FREEDOM THROUGH UNITY"

Lately, I've been guided to write more and more about our relationship to God, and what it means to me. Always, the theme "WE ARE ONE" keeps repeating itself in my mind. Often, I use various analogies to equate our relationship to God: waves upon the Sea of Spirit, snowflakes from the same Cosmic Cloud, apples on the same Tree of Life. In each case, the connection is unbroken. Even in the case of the snowflakes that make a brief sojourn to Earth, ultimately, they will return to the Cloud.

God is FREEDOM, and therefore, so are we. God is UNITY, and therefore, we are all UNITED. The seeming separation between our bodies or between apples on the tree is only an illusion. Once we grow into that awareness, there is absolutely no limit to what we can do while walking the Earth in these vehicles we call bodies.

Jesus, and many others, such as Buddha and Krishna, knew that they were ONE with their SOURCE, our Father/Mother/Creator, and therefore, had all the Power of The Universe within them to be used in service to that SOURCE. We are all Souls that are like chicks emerging from the shell. Once the chicks begin to break through, the world that they knew becomes microscopic compared to the world that awaits. We must break through the shell of our ego's, to catch a glimpse of the LIGHT of our Souls that awaits our AWAKENING. Like the Sun above the clouds, It is always there.

12-11-1989

"WE ARE ONE, WE ARE FREE"

W *HENEVER WE ARE PRONE TO DOUBT, THAT*
E *VERYTHING IS GOING TO WORK OUT,*

A *LL WE NEED TO CALM THAT FEAR, IS*
R *EMEMBER THAT GOD IS "STILL RIGHT HERE"*
E *ACH OF US IS HIS BELOVED CHILD, AND THE*

O *NLY THOUGHT THAT BRINGS A SMILE, IS THAT*
N *OW WE ARE UNITED WITH HIM,*
E *TERNALLY ONE WITH OUR SOURCE WITHIN*

W *HEN WE LIVE THAT THOUGHT EACH DAY,*
E *VERY CLOUD GETS SHINED AWAY,*

A *ND IN ITS PLACE, THERE'S LEFT THE TRUTH, THAT*
R *EMINDS US WE'RE UNFETTERED YOUTHS,*
E *AGER TO ALL THINGS EXPLORE, AND*

F *IND OUT WHAT CREATION'S FOR*
R *EMEMBER OUR FATHER AND YOU ARE FREE,*
E *TERNALLY WALKING WITH HIM, HAPPILY,*
E *TERNALLY ONE WITH HIM, WHO'S LIBERTY!*

12-11-1989

"THE "BE" ATTITUDES"

Beings are those whose material wants are simple,
Because they KNOW that God's Bounty always
Provides them with everything they need, NOW

Beings are those who are never saddened,
Because they KNOW that Joy is their True Source

Beings are those who always follow their Hearts,
Because they KNOW they are doing God's Will

Beings are those who acknowledge only Truth,
Because they KNOW that everything else is an illusion

Beings are those who are forgiving,
Because they KNOW there is nothing to forgive

Beings are those who always manifest God's Love,
Because they KNOW that fear is not Real

Beings are those who are at Peace with all,
Because they KNOW that God is One

12-19-1989

HOW "THE "BE" ATTITUDES" CAME ABOUT

Last month, I was inspired to take each phrase of "A CHILD'S PRAYER", which I wrote while paraphrasing the "OUR FATHER", and match it with the corresponding phrase that Jesus gave during The Sermon On The Mount, providing my current understanding of what that prayer means to me, NOW. By placing both prayers side by side, juxtaposing them, I was able to show the similarities between the two, and bridge the gap of 2,000 years by bringing Jesus' teachings "up to date".

The other great teaching that came from The Sermon On The Mount was "THE BEATITUDES", where Jesus explained how those who are Blessed, (and each one of us is Blessed by our Father. One of Webster's definitions for "Blessed" is: ...Enjoying the Bliss of Heaven...), and conduct their lives accordingly, always have "The Answer" to all of this world's questions. He was demonstrating that if we live according to God's Laws (Lord God, Law of God), then there would never be sorrow, suffering or lack, and only the Abundance and Peace of Heaven.

Each of us is an Eternal Creation of Love, existing as ONE with our Father. Another word for existence is "BEING", and when we acknowledge that we are United with our Creator and are in no way separate from Him, then, we are Living our Lives as the Eternal Beings that God Created. The only cause of sorrow and suffering in this world is the illusion that we are separated from God. It doesn't matter what form the anguish takes, the source of it is the "separation". When we begin to Live our Lives with the attitude that "WE ARE ONE", then, the world begins to dance at our feet, and we KNOW, or are certain, that we are not alone.

In that Light, I was inspired to look at "THE BEATITUDES" and, again, paraphrase them according to my current understanding of what they mean to me, NOW. What was Created during that effort, I have titled "THE "BE" ATTITUDES", and I'll go through the same process as "A CHILD'S PRAYER" by juxtaposing "THE "BE" ATTITUDES" with "THE BEATITUDES".

This will complete my interpretation of The Sermon On The Mount, and I'm very Happy to share it with you. If it helps you to get closer to our Father, then I have served you and Him, along with my True Self, well. WE ARE ONE!

I am also very Happy to be writing this during the One-derful season of Christmas, which signifies the birth of The Christ Child. Each of us is a Cell in the Body of Christ, and when we REMEMBER that, we will, indeed, BE BORN AGAIN. God Bless Us Everyone!

"THE "BE" ATTITUDES"	*"THE BEATITUDES"*
Beings are those whose material wants are simple,	*Blessed are the poor in Spirit:*
Because they KNOW that God's Bounty always provides them with everything they need, NOW	*For theirs is The Kingdom of Heaven*

Jesus always taught simplicity, simplicity, simplicity. He understood that the world which everyone saw, was not the Truth. He knew that scarcity was an illusion, and like all illusions, could be changed. Thus, the "miracle" of the loaves and fishes was His way, not only of feeding 5,000 people but of showing that any form could be changed when one is working with the Universe. Only That which is Eternal is Real and unchangeable. The Beings that we are will always BE PERFECT. The illusions that we believe we are can never be so. The less credence we give to the things of this world, the closer we move towards REMEMBERING our True Selves. Simplicity is the way to release the attachments of this world. God will always provide us with the material needs to sustain our bodies while we are on Earth. Once we REMEMBER Who we are, the world is, as Jesus demonstrated, at our command.

Beings are those who are never saddened,	*Blessed are they that mourn:*
Because they KNOW that Joy is their True Source	*For they shall be comforted*

The ancients used to say: "KNOW THY SELF". To KNOW is to be certain. Each of us has a mind that appears to be split. One part hears only The Voice of Love. The other part hears the voice of fear; the angel and the devil; Christ and anti-Christ. God is Love and Joy, and God is ALL that there is. Anything else is an illusion and has no basis in Reality. Jesus said He would send the Great "Comforter". The Holy Spirit is The Comforter because He hears both voices, and can separate illusion from Truth. He will bring all our illusions to Truth, to let us see them for what they are, thus allowing us to feel SAFE. We can never bring Truth to illusions because Truth is Real and illusions, like dark, heavy clouds, are not. Those ominous clouds could not even support the weight of a pin. Another example would be to believe that an actor who gets shot in a movie really dies. Just because his death appeared very real, and we were emotionally involved in it, didn't change the fact that it was only an illusion (just like the "moving" picture itself is an illusion). It is very easy for us to fall prey to the voice of fear, or our ego. With perception, we see what we want to see. A half glass of water can be half empty or half full, depending on our frame of mind. Thus, if we see someone being killed in "real" life, we think that person is dead because we believe in death. Jesus demonstrated that death is an illusion. God is Life (Light). We are UNITED with That Life, like branches on a tree. REMEMBRANCE of that fact will quickly dispel any fearful, sorrowful thoughts, and return us to a Joyful state.

Beings are those who always follow their Hearts,	*Blessed are the meek:*
Because they KNOW they are doing God's Will	*For they shall inherit the Earth*

There is only One Will in all of Creation, and That is God's Will. In this world, because each of us was given "free will" by our Creator, there appear to be conflicting wills all around us. Thus, the part of our minds that believes it is separate from God, our ego, attempts to do all in its power to maintain the separation between itself and everything and everybody else. On the other hand, the part of our minds that KNOWS It is ONE with God, our True Self or Soul, promotes actions and words that bring us all together and work toward the Good (God) of everyone. Once we learn to recognize the voice of fear and The Voice for God, and heed only That Loving Voice in our Hearts, we can be CERTAIN that we are doing God's Will. Since God is Free, then, so is His Will and ours. Another way of looking at one of Jesus' phrases might be: "For God so Loved the world, that He gave it to His only begotten Son". God has only one Son, and each of us is a Cell in the Body of Christ. The world that God Created is Beautiful. It is only the separate will of humanity that has defiled it. When we are humble or meek enough to relinquish our petty wills to The Will of God, then we shall inherit the Earth and all it has to offer, and return, again, to BEING His Children.

Beings are those who acknowledge only Truth,	*Blessed are they which do hunger and thirst after righteousness:*
Because they KNOW that everything else is an illusion	*For they shall be filled*

What is not Love, is simply fear. In Truth, or Heaven, or Reality, there is only Love. There is no duality or polarity, and everything is ONE, UNITED IN LOVE. In this world that we see, there appear to be choices. We choose between GOOD and evil, JOYOUS and sad, RIGHT and wrong, INNOCENCE and guilt. The part of our minds that is shrouded in the clouds of fear believes in all the negative appearances of this world. The part of our minds that is in THE LIGHT, KNOWS that Love is all there is, and doesn't even acknowledge fear. The Holy Spirit can perceive this world of illusion and KNOWS the True Kingdom of Heaven. He will take each one of our illusions, or dreams of fear, and bring them to Truth so we can "judge" or separate the Truth from the illusion, thus, making the only choice that matters in this world. The "last judgment" is nothing more than our ability to separate, with The Holy Spirit's help, the True from the false. When Light is shined on darkness, the darkness disappears. This is what Jesus meant when He said: "...The Truth shall set you FREE...", for we will be FREED from the chains and darkness of ignorance and fear.

Beings are those who are forgiving,	*Blessed are the merciful:*
Because they KNOW there there is nothing to forgive	*For they shall obtain mercy*

In order for there to be an effect, there must be a cause, since cause equals effect. When Jesus was being beaten, crowned with thorns, scourged, nailed to the cross, and finally, pierced with a spear, His assailants thought they were killing Him. Those actions were the alleged causes of His "death". After the RESURRECTION, when

Jesus' RADIANT BODY was there for all to see, it was obvious that the actions of His executioners had no effect on the body of Jesus. He KNEW that death is an illusion and that is why He asked our Father to forgive His persecutors because, in Truth, there was nothing to forgive. Without an effect, there can be no cause. Thus, in Truth, there is nothing to feel guilty about, because nothing happened. To forgive is to overlook, or forget. When we understand that the un-Loving actions that we perceive others doing are nothing more than illusions, then we will KNOW that there is nothing to forgive. It would be as silly as withholding forgiveness from an actor who played a mass murderer in a movie. We are Eternal Creations of Light (Life), and Light cannot be destroyed (how can Light be attacked?). When we KNOW WE ARE ONE WITH OUR FATHER, we too will be able to calm the winds, heal the sick and even resurrect our own bodies, as Jesus did. He said that all the works He did were through the Father within Him, and that we could do the same works, and more.

Beings are those who always manifest God's Love,	*Blessed are the Pure in Heart:*
Because they KNOW that fear is not Real	*For they shall see God*

When we strive to live God's Law of Love: "...That which you say or do to or for your brother, you say or do to or for your Self...", and really KNOW that the Law is True, then it would be insane to ever do anything fearful to another living Soul again. This is why Jesus taught us to turn the other cheek. He wanted us to give the one striking the blow an opportunity to see that he was really hurting his Self. When we can look at another Child of God and see only Christ's, or God's, face, The Light, where their body is, then we will have found our Selves, because we'll KNOW that we're simply peering into a mirror. When our Hearts are Pure, that is, untainted by any fear, then we are the Love, the SPARKLING DIAMONDS, that God Created. When God had the Thought: "...MY CHILD IS PURE AND HOLY AS I AM...", we came into BEING as extensions of our Father, as UNITED with Him as a wave upon the ocean.

Beings are those who are at Peace with all,	*Blessed are the Peacemakers:*
Because they KNOW that GOD IS ONE	*For they shall be called the Children of God*

How would you treat Jesus if you came face to face with Him? Would you ignore Him, or would you, perhaps, be overwhelmed with great Love for Him? He went through the same trials, was subject to the same temptations and met with the same criticism that each of us is experiencing while Living in this world. He KNEW that THE LIGHT existed beyond the world that He saw, and He didn't let anything or anyone stop Him from reaching His Destiny of lifting the veil of forgetfulness and REMEMBERING HIS TRUE IDENTITY. He overcame the world and saw only Christ's, or God's, Face in every person He met. He KNEW Who He was and Who everyone else was. He KNEW we were all Children of God (Our Father, My Brethren) and that is why He is called "THE PRINCE OF PEACE". He is "THE CHRIST", the Enlightened or Perfected One. Beloved Lord Buddha was also called the Enlightened or Perfected One. They both came to Earth to help us REMEMBER our True Identities, but their messages were not heeded by the majority of the people. Beloved Master Jesus gave us only two commandments: "...LOVE God with all your Heart, Soul, Mind and might, and LOVE your brothers and sisters as you LOVE your True and Radiant Self...". He never gave us any "Thou shalt nots" because He KNEW that everything is LOVE and all else is an illusion. He KNEW then, as He KNOWS NOW, that.......WE ARE LOVE...WE ARE ONE!

"CERTAINTY"

I was inspired to write this little piece so that it could be used as a reminder that, whenever I'm feeling alone or unappreciated.….

GOD KNOWS WHO I AM…

Being human, I still get entangled in the illusions of this world and fall prey to doubt and uncertainty. At those times, God's Voice within my Heart, The Holy Spirit, gently reminds me of The Truth: That I AM as God Created me and am Eternally United with Him. Once again, I am enveloped in God's Peace.

We are all brothers and sisters, and one day, we will AWAKEN and RECOGNIZE each other….God has promised it. That is the True meaning of SALVATION. Have a very Happy and Holy Christmas, and may the new decade be filled with endless Joy and unprecedented Growth. GOD BLESS US EVERYONE!

G *OD IS WHO CREATED US, AND HE'S THE*
O *NE WHO'S LOVE IS SUCH, THAT*
D *ESPITE WHAT OTHERS MAY FORGET, HE*

K *NOWS THAT WE ARE HEAVEN SENT*
N *OW AND THEN THERE COMES A TRAP,*
O *N WHICH WE FAIL TO REMEMBER THAT*
W *E ARE AS GOD CREATED US, AND WE*
S *HINE WITH THE SUN THAT SMILES ABOVE*

W *E MUST AWAKEN FROM THIS DREAM OF FEAR, AND*
H *AVE THE FAITH THAT GOD IS NEAR, AND*
O *NLY WANTS US TO SAY AS ONE:*

I *AM GOD'S BEGOTTEN SON!*

A *LL ELSE SHALL FADE TO NOTHINGNESS, AS THE*
M *IRACLE SHOWS THAT WE ARE BLESSED*

12-22-1989

“THE GOOD SHEPHERD”

The inspiration to write this poem today came after a pleasant half hour in the SUN, during my lunch break. The words...THE GOOD SHEPHERD came to me, so, as I’ve been doing lately, I wrote the words vertically and just let The Holy Spirit within my Soul do Its Thing.

God is THE GOOD SHEPHERD. He KNOWS The Way That is both SAFE and SURE. He is guiding us back HOME after we’ve strayed for so long from our True and Radiant Selves, and our True Reality. This world that we see with our eyes is merely a symbol to help us REMEMBER Who we Really are. That is why Jesus formed so many of His parables with the everyday things that people could relate to.

We need do nothing except have the WILLINGNESS to HEED The Voice in our Hearts and follow It UNCONDITIONALLY, KNOWING that we are being guided exactly where we have to go to BE SAFE, LOVED and ETERNALLY HAPPY.

God is The Conductor, and we are the members of the orchestra, each playing our unique instrument. The Maestro KNOWS how the symphony is to be played, and He directs each musician to that end. They TRUST His Guidance, and the result is PERFECT HARMONY. SO BE IT!

2-08-1990

T *HESE DAYS, I'M DRAWING EVER CLOSER, TO*
H *IM WHO LOVES US OH SO MUCH, THAT*
E *VERY TIME WE HEED HIS WORDS, OUR*

G *OD REJOICES WITH HEAVEN ABOVE. THE*
O *NLY WISH HE HAS FOR US, IS*
O *NENESS WITH ALL OF HIS CREATION,*
D *ESPITE THE THINGS OUR EYES CAN SEE, THEY*

S *HOW ONLY PART OF GOD'S IMAGINATION*
H *E WANTS US TO REMEMBER WHO WE ARE:*
E *TERNAL BEINGS OF LOVE AND TRUTH. WHEN WE*
P *UT OUR TRUST IN HIS DIRECTION, WE*
H *AVE THE PEACE OF INNOCENT YOUTHS*
E *NTER WITH ME IN A HOLY PACT, TO*
R *ELY UPON JUST THE WILL OF GOD*
D *OING SO, WILL ALLOW OUR SELVES TO COMPLETE THEIR*
VERY SPECIAL PARTS

2-08-1990

"EXPECTATIONS"

Yesterday, which was Sunday, March 4, 1990, I watched a movie titled "THE MARATHON MAN". In it, there's a scene where Sir Laurence Olivier's character tells Dustin Hoffman's character that he envied him his college days because it would be the last time that no one expects anything from him. This rang very True with me, as it probably does with many who, for whatever the reason, have spent their Lives doing what others wanted them to do rather than doing what they Really wanted to do.

Many years ago, I bought a plaque with a picture of a cute, sad faced cocker spaniel on it, and underneath the picture, the quote: "...Blessed are they who expect nothing, for they shall not be disappointed...". I didn't Realize at the time how profound those words Truly were, and since I've become AWARE of so much as I continue my AWAKENING, I would NOW add: "...Nor shall they ever be in conflict...".

Thwarted expectations are the chief cause of anger in humans, whether it be something we expect from or for ourselves, or from others. I am at a point in my Life where I have surrendered my need to look outside my Self for anything, be it a job, money, a relationship, Love, approval, Happiness... God is The Source of ALL THAT IS, and I believe He/She/It is at the center of my Being. Therefore, everything springs from The Source within me. This is a huge part of my Truth, and I will do my best to Live my Life according to it, until the evidence that says it is True is so overwhelming, that there is no longer any doubt, and the belief is transformed into KNOWLEDGE, or CERTAINTY ("....The Truth shall set you FREE...").

It's been said that the greatest gift we can give to our Selves is to always do what we want to do, provided we don't deliberately hurt anyone in the process. In other words, that our actions spring from Pure Hearts That are being True to Their True Selves. The greatest gift we can give to another, is to allow them to BE WHO THEY ARE, just as God, through His Grace, allows each one of us to BE who we believe we are, NOW. He KNOWS Who We Really are, and His Love is so great that He allows us to enjoy the REVELATIONS, as we clearly perceive this illusory life for what it is. Like a car's defroster, each of us shall one day melt away the icy veil of forgetfulness with the warmth of our opening Hearts, thereby discovering our True and Radiant Selves.

As I've been doing lately, I write down the phrase that comes to me and then let my True Self Inspire the words that comprise a poem, be it rhyming or not. Today's phrase was…."NO MORE EXPECTATIONS". Much Love to you as we continue our Journey Home.

Your Brother, Michael

3-05-1990

"NO MORE EXPECTATIONS"

N *OW'S THE TIME TO BE TRUE TO MY SELF, WHO'S*
O *NE WITH OUR FATHER AND ALL OF YOU.*

M *ANY TIMES IN MY LIFE, I'VE PLAYED DUBIOUS ROLES,*
O *NLY TO BE LEFT FEELING THERE WAS MORE TO FULFILLMENT.*
R *IGHT NOW, I JUST WANT TO BE ME, WITH NO*
E *XPECTATIONS TO LIVE UP TO, FROM EITHER ME OR YOU.*

E *VERYTHING IN THIS LIFE IS MEANT TO REVEAL THE TRUTH, AS AN*
X *RAY SHOW'S WHAT'S HIDDEN BENEATH THE SURFACE.*
P *ARTS THAT I'VE PLAYED WITH MY FELLOW ACTORS, HAVE*
E *DUCATED ME AS TO WHO'S THE REAL ME, INSPIRING ME TO*
C *ALL ON HIM FOR ALL OF MY NEEDS.*
T *O GOD, I AM PERFECT, AS SHE CREATED ME,*
A *ND THAT TRUTH IS REVEALED MORE AND MORE EACH DAY.*
T *O HIM I SURRENDER MY PETTY, LITTLE will, BECAUSE*
I *KNOW THAT HIS WILL IS THE ONLY ONE THERE IS.*
O *N MY JOURNEY HOME, I'LL SHARE WHAT I'M LEARNING,*
N *OT SPARING GOD'S LOVE, WHICH*
S *PRINGS ETERNAL FROM DEEP WITHIN MY HEART*

Thank You, My Beloved

“THE INANITY OF the ego”

March 6, 1990, marked my completion of the 365th, and final, lesson in “A COURSE IN MIRACLES”, a ONE-derful book designed to help us REMEMBER our True Identities by ALLOWING The Holy Spirit within us to separate God’s Truth from man’s illusion.

The cornerstone of The Course is: WE ARE AS GOD CREATED US, and it’s only our belief that we are a self that’s separated from God that keeps us mired (maya’d*) in this world of illusion. That self is the ego/personality (from the Latin “persona” meaning mask), which is something each of us begins making from birth and is Really a substitute for our True Selves, or The God within. God Created (Creation is Eternal, while the things that we make are temporary) us in His/Her/Its Image and Likeness (Lightness) and That is ALL that He sees. The Perfection That is ONE with Him will always BE so, but the part of our minds that believes it is separated from God, that fearful thought known as the ego, believes only in separation, discord, fear, sorrow, scarcity, sickness and, of course, death. Everything that the ego believes is the exact opposite of what’s True in Reality, just as hell is the opposite of Heaven.

Thinking about the ego the other night, I was reminded of Bram Stoker’s literary creation, Count Dracula. The more I thought of the similarities between the ego and the Count, the more I was convinced that Stoker was in-Spired to pen this allegory of Good and evil to help us better understand the part of our minds that still believes it is separated from God.

I was in-Spired to juxtapose (ala “A CHILD’S PRAYER” and “THE “BE” ATTITUDES”) the similarities between good ol’ Count Dracula and our own abortive creation, the ego, and let The Holy Spirit work through my personality. So, without further ado, here’s:

“THE INANITY OF the ego”

*Maya is a Sanskrit word referring to the cosmic illusion that the ONENESS of ALL Creation is separated into countless pieces that appear to be physical reality, while ignoring the “invisible” energy that is its source. It is like saying that the Light from a candle on a cake is separated from the Light emanating from the other candles.

With Love, Your Brother, Michael 3-09-1990

"THE COUNT"	***"the ego"***
Fear of Light	*Fear of Truth*

Dracula only mingled with the world under the cover of darkness, and was terrified at the thought of being caught out in the SUN. The ego is also afraid of The Light, or Truth, and thrives on lies (Jesus referred to Satan as "a liar"). It believes that its whole existence is based on perpetuating the illusion of separation between bodies and that the body is, indeed, the reality of who we are. Jesus said that He was The Light of the world, and He proved that the body was not His True Identity, but merely a vehicle for Him to use in performing God's Work on while on Earth.

Fear of the crucifix	*Fear of God*

As Dracula was repulsed by the sight of the cross, so is the ego repulsed by any reference to God, or Good, be It Thought, Word or Deed. The ego believes that its existence depends on discouraging us from following our Hearts or Spirits, and it does all in its "power" to prevent us from doing so. For example, it is the ego's voice that tries to dissuade us from calling someone we haven't seen for awhile by giving us numerous reasons why we shouldn't call that person, right after our Spirit gives us the suggestion to do so. An easy way to understand the concept is to picture an Angel on one of our shoulders, and a devil on the other (remember Porky Pig?). It's up to each of us to recognize the 2 voices and then CHOOSE which one we're always going to heed. Since they contradict each other, they both can't be True.

Feeds on others' blood	*Feeds on others*

The vampire existed by draining the blood, or Life Force, from its victims. It depended on others for its very existence, and was always looking for new sources upon whom to prey. Again, it walked the Earth in constant fear, wondering where its next meal was coming from. The same is true for ego's that also feed off others. They like to drain people's enthusiasm (from the Greek "theus", for God , hence, the God within) by dumping their fears and concerns on them, but aren't interested in helping others with their problems. They are possessive of a lover or mate for fear that they will lose the source of their happiness. They like to take, but never give, unless it serves their own self interest. Like the Count, they live their lives in fear that the supply will some day run out. Many nations wage wars for the same illusory reason. Because the ego believes it is separated from God, it always looks outside itself for what it needs, rather than turning to The Source That is Actually within. Jesus demonstrated that, when we acknowledge that WE ARE ONE with God, we can, through The Infinite Power of God within us, feed thousands with very little.

Changed form *Inconsistent*

Besides appearing as the suave Count, Dracula could also change into a bat and a wolf, both creatures that thrived in the darkness. So too, does the ego seem to have split personalities in dealing with people. One minute, it can be happy and enthused, and the next, it can be sad and depressed. With an ego, one never knows what's next, or what its reaction is going to be in a given situation. James Cagney once played a ruthless character named Cody Jarrett, in a movie titled "WHITE HEAT". Cody wouldn't think twice about killing someone in cold blood, but he'd get a tear in his eye when he thought of his beloved mother. He was a classic example of a split mind. With God, we KNOW His Love for us is both PURE, that is, untainted by fear, and SURE, or Certain. We can never have a Truly Loving experience with an ego, because its brand of love is based on fear. Give to it, but don't expect to receive anything Real in return. Where God's Love is UNCONDITIONAL, the ego places innumerable conditions on its love. It will love you if you change, or stop doing something it doesn't like, or jump through a few hoops, etc.

Controls victims *Thrives on control*

Bela Lugosi was famous for his line: "Look into my eyes!". He was able to control the will of those under his spell and have them do his bidding. The same is true for ego's that are most comfortable when they are in a position of control. The other side of the coin, for them, is the constant fear in which they exist because they may, at any time, lose the control, or hold, they have over those in their circle. Where the ego never allows others to BE WHO THEY ARE, God always allows us our free will, just as an Enlightened Soul will always ALLOW others to BE WHO THEY ARE....NOW.

No reflection in a mirror	*Is an illusory self*

One way the vampire hunters could determine a creature's identity would be to see if it produced an image when it was in front of a mirror. If they couldn't see a reflection, they got their stakes and hammers ready for a raid at sunrise. The same is true for an ego, which is merely the part of one's mind that believes it is separated from God. It is a figment of our imagination and does not exist in Reality. When a person suffers from amnesia and believes he or she is someone else, those who knew the person before, KNOW who that person really is and just wait and try to help them remember their true identity. God KNOWS WHO we are because She Created us. He also is waiting for us to AWAKEN AND REMEMBER OUR TRUE IDENTITIES, Which never stopped BEING ONE WITH HIM/HER. The Atonement, or AT-ONE-MENT, is nothing more than a correction to our minds, reminding us that the selves we thought we were never existed in Reality; that we always have been and always will BE ONE WITH OUR CREATOR.

Exists in constant fear	*Exists in constant fear*

As has been demonstrated throughout this discussion, every moment of the Count's existence was fraught with fear. Fear of running out of victims, fear of losing control, fear of discovery, fear of SUNLIGHT, fear of its own death, fear of God, fear, fear, fear. The ego too, is nothing more than a fearful thought. In this world, all the emotions can be boiled down to two categories: Love based and fear based. If a thought, word or deed does not have Love as its Source, then it is fear based. If God is Peace, Love and Truth, then everything that is not Peace, Love and Truth must be conflict, fear and illusion, having no existence in

God's Reality (That would explain why the Sun kept shining and the Earth kept spinning in the face of humanity's most heinous atrocities). Just as a dream is not Real and occurs only when we are sleeping, so too, does the ego's world, the world of illusion, not exist in Reality, or Heaven, and only seems real while we remain asleep, or suffering from amnesia.

Destroy with stake through the heart *Disappears with opening Heart*

Most of us know how the Count was dispatched, a sharp stake through his heart and he disintegrated into dust, never to be seen again. The same is true for the ego. As our Hearts open and we listen to God's Voice, The Voice of the Angel instead of the devil, the ego loses its power. When Light is shined on darkness, the darkness disappears, and in Truth, was never there. The part of our minds that believes it is separated from God is merely shrouded in dark, heavy clouds, which when burned away, reveal the Infinitely vast blue sky and Brilliant Sun, which have always been there.

Repulsed by the aroma of garlic *Repulsed by the sweetness in others*

To keep the vampire away from a potential victim while he or she slept, a necklace of garlic was placed around the neck of the individual. For some reason, the pungent aroma of the garlic was repulsive to those tortured Souls, and they looked elsewhere for a meal. Ego's too, seem to be repulsed by the aromatic sweetness that other Souls express through their personalities. They will look at a positive, upbeat personality and criticize them for perhaps being phony, or too good to be true. After they secretly criticize that person behind their back, the ego will most likely avoid them....birds of a feather, and all that. I once purchased a tee shirt that had a picture of a group of black sheep in the center, and off to the side, one lonely white sheep. Beneath the picture was the caption: "....It's tough being the black sheep of the family....". Ego's are repulsed by those who are not negative and dis-Spirited like they are. I guess in their case, misery does, indeed, love company. Once those ego's start to AWAKEN, they'll see that: WE ALL ARE WHITE SHEEP!

There is so much more that can be said. Perhaps you'll add some of your own ideas to the foregoing, but for now I'm sharing this with you to help make you aware of the split minds that each of us has. There is not now, nor has there ever been, a Soul on this planet who did not face the same battle that each of us is waging. Jesus fought his ego right until the moment that He "died" on the cross. In the garden at Gethsemane, on the night before the crucifixion, He got angry at His disciples for not staying awake and praying with Him. While praying to His Father, He expressed His fear by asking that, if It were God's Will, He not have to endure the upcoming ordeal. While hanging on the cross, He expressed His despair and sense of separation from God when He said: "Father, why hast Thou forsaken me?". It wasn't until He said: "It is finished" that He KNEW that He'd won His battle with the ego. He KNEW then, that the ego existed no longer and that He would RESURRECT and assume His True Identity as The Christ, or God, manifested on Earth in flesh and blood.

Jesus' Life was a symbol and example for us to learn from and Live by. Each of our selves must "die" in order to be reborn as The Christ. As Jesus went through His cleansing process, so too must each of us cleanse our Hearts of all fear and negativity. When we can look upon each person that we meet as our SINLESS, INNOCENT BROTHER instead of a sinful, guilty ego, we will have achieved SALVATION, which is REMEMBRANCE OF GOD. On the day we can see Christ's, or God's, Face as The Light in all whom we meet, we will have AWAKENED, because we will KNOW that we are simply peering into a mirror, and, unlike the Count, are gazing upon the Perfect Reflection That is Lovingly gazing back.

"MIKEY STARSEED"

This is the first poem I've written since compiling "THE LAMPLIGHTER", and it's fitting that I was in-Spired to write it now, 11 days before I leave for Tibet.

Jesus has said that we must be as "little children" to enter The Kingdom of Heaven, and these past 2 weeks I've been working with the child part of my Being. The Souls of each of us are comprised of 3 parts; the male part, which is Powerful and Wise; the female part, which is Loving, Compassionate and Nurturing; and the child part, which is Innocent, Trusting, Creative, Unlimited and Playful. The child of my Being has been neglected for a long, long time, and it's appropriate NOW for it to come to the surface and unite the Triad of my Spirit.

In my pre-"AWAKENING" days, people who knew me or worked with me used to call me "Mikey". I liked it because I felt like a kid during those times. I always enjoyed the story of "JOHNNY APPLESEED", who used to walk the land planting apple seeds wherever he went, not waiting for them to grow, but confident that they would.

At this point in my Life, I want to walk the Earth, planting seeds of Light, Star Seeds, in the minds of people I meet, by reminding them, through my example, that WE ARE AS GOD CREATED US and nothing will ever change that fact. Because God has Willed that His Children AWAKEN and return HOME to Him, like Johnny Appleseed, I too am confident that the seeds I plant will also germinate, take root and grow. So, without further ado, heeeeeere's Mikey!

M *OVED TO HELP MY BROTHERS SEE,*
I *ONLY WANT TO MANIFEST ME*
K *NOWING, FULL WELL, THAT GOD IS ONE,*
E *TERNALLY, I AM HIS BELOVED SON*
Y *ET, SO ARE YOU, AND ALL OF US, WE*

S *IBLINGS OF TRUTH, AND LIGHT, AND LOVE*
T *O ME, MY PLEASURE IS PLANTING SEEDS,*
A *LLOWING THEM TO GROW INTO STRONG, TALL TREES*
R *ATHER THAN WAIT AND WATCH THEM GROW, I'M*
S *AFE IN THE KNOWLEDGE THAT ALL WILL FLOW, WHEN*
E *ACH SEED BEGINS TO GERMINATE, AND*
E *VERY SOUL STARTS TO DEMONSTRATE, THE*
D *IVINELY PERFECT FRUITS OF THEIR TREES, THAT WERE*
PLANTED BY ME, LITTLE MIKEY STARSEED!

4-07-1990

"YES"

Recently, my very good friend and mentor, Beloved Master Merlin, shared something with me that I'd like to share with you. He explained how powerful the word "YES" is, and how important it was to use that word more and more in our daily lives. As with everything He's shared with me over these past 3 ½ years, His words felt very True to me and so, I began to look at them by tuning in to God's Voice within my Heart, and listen to What He said about "YES".

Through God's Grace, we were Created and have our Being, Eternally United with Him, Free to Be His ambassadors of Love throughout the world. He asks only that we not intentionally harm anyone in the process of discovering Who we are, or attempt to take away another's God given Free will. Oftentimes, others will misunderstand our actions because of their current understanding and perceptions, but as long as our actions spring from Pure Hearts, their misunderstanding is not our responsibility. In this world, there is always another way of looking at, or perceiving, a particular individual or situation. Each Soul is responsible for Its Own growth.

With God, everything else is YES! YES to Life, YES to Love, YES to Unity, YES to Sharing, YES to Caring, YES to Creating, YES to Experiencing, YES to Learning, YES to Teaching, YES to Being. YES! YES! YES! She wants us to Be Happy with Her Forever, and to AWAKEN from this AMNESIA that we've existed, certainly not Really Lived, in for far too long.

I recently returned from a trip to Tibet, where I had the most ONE-derful, ONE-drous experience of my Life. I saw, with my own eyes, that which I've always known in my Heart.....that people all over the world are, indeed, God's Children. Inside their bodies and Souls is that Spark of Divinity that yearns to Be ex-pressed (pressed out) through acts of Love. Whether I was in mainland China, or high in the Himalaya's, the True Essence of the people I met was the same.....

Sparkling eyes and Bright smiles. I beheld God's Face in each of them, and I am Eternally Grateful to our Creator for the experience.

Getting back to "YES". I started looking at the word itself, to see if the sound of it had any particular meaning or feeling for me. At first, I thought of YEA, as in yea or nay. That reminded me of the exclamation YAY! What Joyous images that word evokes. Children playing, the landing on the Moon, the birth of a child, winning the World Series, the end of a war between nations, being hired on to a much desired job. Add your own Joyous images, as with "THE INANITY OF the ego", the list could, like the "Energizer" bunny, just keep going.

So, for me, the word in English resounded of Joy. Certainly, God is Joy. I thought it would be fun to look at the way YES is expressed in other languages and see where it went. Here are a few other forms of YES from around the world:

Italian, Spanish	SI, pronounced SEE. With God, we can Truly SEE everything as it is, and not as it seems.
French	OUI, pronounced WE. With God, WE ARE ONE, and are not separated in any way.
Japanese	HAI, pronounced HIGH. With God, everything is of the HIGHEST ORDER and comes from the HIGHEST SOURCE.
German	JA, pronounced YAH. With this word, I was reminded of JOY and also the Hebrew word for God...YAHWEH.
Mandarin Chinese	SUH, pronounced as I've spelled it. The pronunciation reminded me of SURE, as God's Love for us is SURE.
Thai	KRUP, pronounced as I've spelled it. The word CROP came to mind. God's Bounteous CROP of gifts is available to each of us once we say YES to Her/Him.

Hindi	HAAN, pronounced HAHN. I thought of HAH, HAH, HAH. With God, Laughter is the order of the day.
Russian	DA, pronounced DAH. That reminded me of a toddler's DA DA, when referring to its father. God is our Father.
Filipino	O, pronounced OH. Again, I was reminded of OH HO and HO, HO, HO. This is more Fun than I thought it would be!

YES....for me....another way of saying.......God!

Tune in to your True and Radiant Self and let It help you learn to say YES, YES, YES! The time for "no" is over. The Truth shall set us FREE!!

Love, Your Brother

Michael (AKA: "Mikey Starseed")

6-30-1990

"INSPIRATION"

It's been awhile since I was in-Spired to write a piece that had Spiritual Growth as its theme. Much has occurred in my Life since my last co-Creation, which is titled: "YES", and was written on 6-30-1990.

After my trip to Tibet and China last April, I went about the business of releasing more of my old attachments and resolving my longstanding relationships with my ex-wife and my former girlfriend. I also found Harmony with my three "children", as well as experiencing the "Peace that passeth understanding" of which Beloved Master Jesus spoke.

In between all that, I found my Beloved Elspeth on 5-30-1990, went through an accelerated courtship which resulted in my meeting her a month later in London, and our forming a Spiritual Union on the train to Glasgow, Scotland on July 4, 1990. I moved out of my apartment in Westlake, Ca. and in with her at the end of September.

While I wrote many beautiful words of Love for her during that time, there was no in-Spiration to write anything concerning "The Path" that I have chosen....until yesterday. While languishing* through a lesson that my True Self presented me concerning my continued personality purification, I wrote the word "INSPIRATION" vertically and the following evolved:

I *S THE BODY WHO I AM? I THINK*
N *OT. IS THE*
S *OUL WHO I AM?*
P *ERHAPS.....*
I *KNOW THAT I AM MORE THAN IS*
R *EVEALED TO THE PHYSICAL EYES,*
A *ND I*
T *RUST THAT ALL MY TEACHERS' WISDOM HAS*
I *NSPIRED ME TO FOLLOW THE*
O *NE, TRUE PATH THAT LEADS TO*
N *IRVANA**, AND UNION WITH MY CREATOR!*

*I find it interesting that Webster defines "languish" as being "dis-spirited" and I was in-Spired to write this. Thank You, my Beloved Self.

**Webster defines "Nirvana" as "...The final beatitude that transcends suffering...and is sought, especially in Buddhism, through the extinction of desire and individual (ego) consciousness...."

10-16-1990

"REMEMBRANCE"

When I consciously began my Spiritual AWAKENING nearly 4 years ago, my personality was at a familiar place, asking the Eternal questions: "...Who am I...Why am I...Where am I going...?". Much has occurred since then, and my personality has been taught many lessons. A great deal of what I've been learning (or more accurately, un-learning and remembering) has been recorded in my two books, "BABYSTEPS" and "THE LAMPLIGHTER".

Along "The Way", I Realized that my Soul was the One with the Destiny, and God's Voice within my Soul, That Spark of Divinity That each of us was Created with, KNOWS exactly Who I AM, Why I AM here and Where I AM going. As I learned to listen to That Voice more and more, and ignore the frightened voice of my ego/personality, I grew more Trusting and hence, more Peaceful.

As I continued to AWAKEN, my wants became less and less, and soon, all I Really wanted was to REMEMBER my True Identity and share that adventure with my "Golden Girl", a Soul in a female body who wanted the same thing. Well, on May 30, 1990, Memorial Day (how fitting), I was reunited with my Beloved Elspeth. Now we are two joined in God's Name, and we both want to return Home with REMEMBRANCE of our True Identities. I believe that God's Plan for Salvation is simply that: AWAKENING from our sleep of fear and separation from Him, and Remembering God and our Unity (AT-ONE-MENT) with Him/Her.

The Creative Juices have started to flow again, and here is my second co-Creation in as many days........REMEMBRANCE:

R *EMEMBERING MY BELOVED CREATOR IS*

E *VERYTHING THAT I LIVE FOR THESE DAYS.*

M *Y ENDS HAVE BEEN REDUCED TO THIS ONE, NOW THAT*

E *LSPETH IS WITH ME AGAIN.*

M *Y BELOVED HELPS ME TO*

B *ECOME SHINY, SPARKLY BY*

R *EFLECTING BACK TO ME ALL THAT I AM, AND*

A *LL THAT I'M NOT. AS I REMOVE THAT WHICH I'M*

N *OT, WHAT REMAINS IS THE*

C *RYSTAL, PURE CREATION THAT IS*

E *TERNALLY ONE WITH ITS CREATOR!*

AUM, AMEN and SO BE IT!

10-17-1990

"CONFIRMATION"

This piece completes the trilogy that began 2 days ago with "INSPIRATION". I HAVE been in-Spired these past days, and it feels very, very Good to be in touch with my Self via these writings. Doing so always draws me closer to God and ALL THAT IS. Beloved Master Jesus once said: "....By their fruits you shall know them...". "A COURSE IN MIRACLES" takes that a step further by adding: "....and they shall know themselves...". If we are Eternal Creations of Light and Love, Created by our Father to "BE" One with Him and all Creation Forever, then our bodies are not the Truth of Who we are, since they are very fragile and temporary.

The "Course" also teaches that one way to SALVATION, or REMEMBRANCE of God and our True Selves, is by means of the "HOLY RELATIONSHIP". Unlike an unholy, or ego/body based relationship, the Holy, or God/Spirit based Relationship, leads us away from fear, pain, darkness and death, and back towards Love, Peace, Light and Eternal Life, which are part of our True birthright. Our partner in the Holy Relationship reflects back to us whatever we send out. Whether we project fear and darkness, or Love and Light, it will be reflected back, as if we were standing before a mirror. Through this Relationship, we are able, if we have the desire, willingness and courage to accept responsibility for all that we are, to cleanse our personalities of all that God did not Create, and become the SHINY, SPARKLING Beings that He Created in His/Her Image. Some of Webster's definitions for shiny and sparkling are: "...filled with light, bright in appearance, polished;...to give off or reflect bright moving points of light...".

Beloved Master Jesus manifested His Light body to some of His disciples, and because He said He was the Life, the Truth and the Way, I believe that each of us must ultimately evolve into the example He modeled for us. I KNOW that God has brought my Beloved Elspeth and me together at this time because we both want to "BE" as God Created us. Together, by following the Guidance of God's Holy Spirit

That dwells within each of us, we will become, as my Beloved friend and teacher once said, "…oh so shiny, sparkly…".

Back in the '60's, there was a song titled: "AQUARIUS, LET THE SUN SHINE IN". I'd like to write one titled: "ALL OF US, LET GOD'S SON SHINE OUT". I believe that each of us is a cell in the body of Christ, or God ex-pressed through flesh and blood.

God Bless "All of Us" as we continue our journey back Home to Him/Her….together. Here's the latest in-Spiration that I'd like to share with you, it's titled: "CONFIRMATION".

With deep Love, your brother, Michael

10-18-1990

"CONFIRMATION"

C *AN ONE TRULY KNOW*

O *NE'S SELF? I BELIEVE IT IS*

N *OT ONLY POSSIBLE, BUT ABSOLUTELY NECESSARY.*

F *OR, AWAKENING FROM THIS DREAM OF FEAR,*

I *BELIEVE, IS GOD'S PLAN FOR OUR SALVATION.*

R *EMEMBRANCE OF OUR TRUE SELVES WILL*

M *ANIFEST THROUGH OUR BROTHERS*

A *ND SISTERS. AS*

T *HEY ACKNOWLEDGE THE LIGHT THAT*

I *S IN US, WE KNOW THAT IT'S THERE.*

O *UR JOB IS TO CLEANSE OUR PERSONALITIES OF ALL*

N *EGATIVITY, AND WHAT REMAINS IS... THE TRUTH!*

WE ARE AS GOD CREATED US!

THANK YOU, FATHER

"THE LIGHT OF THE WORLD"

When I penned the poem "THE LAMPLIGHTER", back in April of 1989, I made reference to Jesus' statement that He was the Light of the world, and, because He also said that He was the Truth and the Way, the same was True of us. We, also, are Lights of the world. If we are as God Created us, perfect Beings of Light and Love, then, the body/personality is not Who we are, and it is up to each of us to Reveal God's Eternal Flame That dwells within our Souls. As Jesus also exemplified, this is accomplished by cleansing the personality of all false beliefs and negativity and allowing That Light to shine forth.

In the day to day nitty gritty, it is often difficult to keep our True Identities in the forefront of our conscious minds. We see people who are sad, mad or un-Loving. We read about war, killing and poisoning of the planet. As hard as we might try, or as Good as we want to Be, most of us succumb each day to the illusion, or darkness, of this world. The thought occurred to me this morning that this world, because of its darkness, gives those of us who are in the process of AWAKENING, an opportunity to Really shine forth. Just as a candle is best seen in the darkness, so too must we allow our Eternal Flames to Be Beacons of Hope to a weary, frightened world that is shrouded in the clouds of fear and ignorance. Through our very existence, we will refute the teaching of this world by demonstrating another Way of Living. As noted in earlier writings, when Light is shined on darkness, the darkness disappears. The Truth shall, indeed, set all of us Free.

Let us continue to Be the Truth That God Created. Let us ever strive to REMEMBER our True Homes and our True Estate, and not believe in the falsity of this shadow world. Either we are as God Created us, or we are not. We cannot change the Truth about Who we are, but we can change our belief about who and what we think we are. I am going to continue my quest, with the help of my Beloved Elspeth, by removing that which God did not Create. Elspeth is, for me, like a superfine filter that allows only Light to pass through it. I believe that when the last imperfection has been Revealed to me and I release it, then God's

Light will shine forth unobstructed in all Its Radiant Glory. You are all my Brothers and Sisters in The Light, and I welcome you to join me in returning Home, in consciousness, to our Creator. SO BE IT!

Following this narrative is my latest in-Spiration that I wrote during lunch hour, using the words "THE LIGHT OF THE WORLD" as a frame. As Tiny Tim said in "A CHRISTMAS CAROL"…"...God bless us… everyone!…".

With Love and Affection,
Michael

10-29-1990

"THE LIGHT OF THE WORLD"

T *O BECOME WHO GOD CREATED, I BELIEVE,*
H *AS GOT TO BE THE*
E *TERNAL DESTINY OF EACH OF US.*

L *ESS THAN THAT*
I *MPLIES THAT*
G *OD, WHO IS PERFECT, CREATES IMPERFECTION.*
H *E KNOWS THE*
T *RUTH ABOUT US, AND*

O *NLY WANTS HIS WAYWARD CHILDREN TO RETURN HOME TO THEIR*
F *ATHER.*

T *HIS IS ACCOMPLISHED BY REMEMBERING THAT THE KINGDOM OF*
H *EAVEN IS WITHIN*
E *ACH OF US. THE SPARK OF DIVINITY*

W *ITHIN OUR SOULS IS THE ETERNAL FLAME THAT, DAY*
O *R NIGHT, IS SHINING BRIGHTLY. AS WE*
R *EMOVE THE LAYERS OF NEGATIVITY FROM OUR PERSONALITIES, THE*
L *IGHT OF THE WORLD SHINES FORTH,*
D *ECLARING OUR ONENESS WITH OUR CREATOR!*

“FISHERS OF MEN”

F *REEDOM FROM THE PAIN AND SORROW OF THIS WORLD*
I *S A GOAL THAT MOST FEEL IS ATTAINED ONLY THROUGH DEATH.*
S *O MUCH OF WHAT I’VE BEEN LEARNING AFFIRMS THAT*
H *EAVEN IS WITHIN US, AND THEREFORE, WITHIN OUR REACH, NOW.*
E *ACH OF US WAS CREATED AS PERFECT*
R *EFLECTIONS OF GOD, AND OUR RESPONSIBILITY IS TO*
S *CRUB AWAY THE JUNK THAT GOD DID NOT CREATE, BUT WE MADE.*

O *NCE WE ACCOMPLISH THAT, WE CAN BECOME GOD’S*
F *ISHERS, LURING ALL TO HEAVEN WITH THE BAIT OF FORGIVENESS.*

M *ANY OF US ARE TANGLED IN OUR “ego-self” NETS OF MISERY, AND*
E *ACH TIME WE WITHHOLD FORGIVENESS FROM US OR ANOTHER, WE*
N *EGATE OUR TRUE SELVES AND TRUE REALITY, WHICH IS HEAVEN.*

11-07-1990

I was in-Spired to write the foregoing today to underline the importance of forgiveness in our Lives. Jesus taught many lessons, but the greatest of them was the necessity and the power of forgiveness. He KNEW His True Identity, as well as Ours, and He expressed that understanding when He declared: "…I and My Father are One…". He healed the sick by telling them that their sins were forgiven and to sin no more. He gave us the Perfect example of forgiveness when He compassionately forgave His persecutors, who mocked Him to the very end of His ordeal on the cross.

Sin is separation from God, Who is Love, and Love is ALL THERE IS. Forgiveness is unnecessary in Heaven, or Reality, but in this illusory world of God substitutes, or ego/personalities, it is required to free up the frozen energy in our Beings that acts like a magnet to attract the same thing that is not forgiven. It is the one illusion that does not lead to another illusion. It is the only way out of this maze of confusion and separation from God. When He was asked how it was possible to forgive 7 times a day, Beloved Master Jesus replied that it wasn't necessary to forgive 7 times (smile), but rather, 70 times 7, as God forgives us all of our countless transgressions every day.

Through forgiveness, Peace will be returned to our awareness, and the Memory of God will Shine forth in our minds. With God's Memory restored to us, our True Identities will be REMEMBERED, and everything and everyone we look upon will be BEAUTIFUL and PURE. SO BE IT! THANK YOU, MY BELOVED SELF.

"DO EVERYTHING WITH JOY"

D *ISREGARDING*
O *UR LITTLE,*

E *go wills IS*
V *ITAL TO OUR*
E *NTERING THE KINGDOM WHILE STILL IN OUR BODIES. THE*
R *IFT BETWEEN THE ego's fearful voice, AND GOD'S VOICE IN MY AND*
Y *OUR HEARTS IS*
T *HE SOURCE OF ALL CONFLICT IN OUR LIVES.*
H *EAVEN, OR LOVE,*
I *S THE ONLY REALITY,*
N *OW AND FOREVER.*
G *OD IS THE CREATOR OF LOVE AND SHE HAS DEFINED*

W *HAT LOVE MEANS. ONE OF*
I *TS QUALITIES IS JOY, OR BLISS. A WAY, FOR ME,*
T *O ALWAYS LIVE ACCORDING TO GOD'S WILL IS TO RESPOND TO*
H *IS VOICE AS IF MY SOUL WERE PRESENT AS HE SPOKE. THIS ALLOWS*

J *OY TO BE THE BASIC EMOTION IN ALL MY ACTIONS; FROM MY*
O *CCUPATION AT WORK, TO SHARING MY LOVE WITH*
Y *OU AND ALL MY BROTHERS AND SISTERS, EVERY CHANCE I GET.*

THANK YOU, MY BELOVED SELF

11-09-1990

When I was in-Spired, last year, to paraphrase "THE BEATITUDES", the Creation that evolved was titled "THE "BE" ATTITUDES". One of the "BE" attitudes (ego's have attitudes, Spirits do not) is:

"Beings are those Who are never saddened,

Because they KNOW that Joy is their True Source"

As I continue the relinquishment of my ego to my Spirit, or Soul, by cleansing my personality of all false beliefs and negativity, I am NOW challenged with the opportunity of always living this particular "BE" attitude. I have been unhappy most of my Life with almost every job I've ever had. Laziness was not the issue, but rather, dissatisfaction with the work I was doing.

I've since learned that everything I've experienced in my Life has been necessary to prepare me for what I am to do to fulfill my Soul's Destiny, but still, my ego tries its best to sidetrack me. My ego's little will, or "little willy", is losing its hold on me once and for all.

The other day, God's Voice in my Heart asked me to imagine how I'd respond if my Soul appeared before me and asked me to stay at my current job until He asked me to move on (I saw this years ago in a movie with Jon Voight....can't remember the title). Of course my reply would be a resounding YES!

What would your response be? C'mon...Let's go Home.... together!

Love, Michael

"10"

Seek not outside your Self…
For any thing

Be Joyful when you speak or hear your Creator's Name…
It is yours as well

Remember that…
You are ONE with your Father

Acknowledge that God, your Creator…
Is your Wise and Powerful Father,
As well as your Loving, Nurturing Mother

Allow your brothers to Be Who they are NOW…
And Revere all Life

Share God's bounty…
For, all are ONE

Strive to keep your Heart Pure…
As It was Created

Stay in Integrity by always…
Thinking, speaking and Living the Truth,
As you understand It

Know that you are complete…
Through your Creator

Realize that you always have what you need…
NOW

6-27-1991

AN INTRODUCTION TO "10"

Welcome back! I say that not to you, but to that ONE-derful feeling I get when the urge to Create begins to course through my Being. As it was with the most recent cycle of writings that appeared last Fall, it has been quite awhile since I've written any "LAMPLIGHTER" type pieces. This project has been on my mind for more than a year. Shortly after I wrote "A CHILD'S PRAYER" and "THE "BE" ATTITUDES", paraphrasing them with "THE OUR FATHER" and "THE BEATITUDES", I got the idea to do the same thing with "THE TEN COMMANDMENTS". I mused over what to title the work and what ideas I would try to convey.

That was happening in April of 1990, shortly before I left for Tibet. Upon my return, as I documented in many of last Fall's writings, I went about the business of tying the loose ends of my old life, and nurturing the tender shoots of my new one. For the last year, my Beloved Elspeth and I have grown closer to God, our Selves and each other. The most important thing for me was to learn to Love my Beloved unconditionally, as I Loved my True and Radiant Self. My Love for God grew enormously in the year prior to my meeting Elspeth. In fact, after returning from Tibet, I had accepted the possibility that I would not meet my "Golden Girl", and that I would go the rest of The Way only with God, and not with another Soul joined with me in God's Name. Two days after that acceptance, I met my Beloved. Thank You, Father.

So, why am I writing today? Because it feels right. The seeds were planted last year, the ideas have developed and grown in my Heart and the words are NOW ready to be reaped. I say this with absolute Trust that, never knowing exactly what will be written, I do KNOW that God's Voice within my Heart will pass on exactly what needs to be shared. (As it turned out, I wrote this entire piece in one day, with very few changes.)

Moses received "The Ten Commandments" 3,000 years ago, at a time when mankind was in a very carnal, darkened state. Although many of today's events would indicate that the situation hasn't changed a great deal, I believe that we are AWAKENING Children of God Who are beginning to suspect that we are more than meets the physical eye. We do not need to be controlled by a bunch of Thou Shalt Nots, but rather we must learn to listen to God's Voice and be guided by it until the moment that we BECOME His Voice. For me, my only desire is conscious REMEMBRANCE of God, and then Being a Shining Light that others can use to help find their Way out of the darkness (The Buddhists refer to those Souls as Boddhisatva's). Adios for NOW, and GOD BLESS US EVERYONE!

Your Brother, Michael

6-27-1991

I AM the Lord, thy God, thou shalt not have Strange gods before Me

Seek not outside your Self... For any thing

Two years ago, on 6-26-1989, at a time when I was experiencing much pain in my Life, Beloved Master Merlin advised me that "...It is time to set aside these falsenesses that claim to be important...". He was referring to my job situation and all the turmoil I was experiencing because of my conflict with it. I understood His meaning immediately because the only thing that mattered was Being True to my True Self, That Spark of Divinity Which is The Christ within you and me. That is the Real, or Eternal, part of our Beings. Everything in this world is temporary and will disappear when time is no more. Material possessions, money, superficial relationships, power, position, etc. are the false gods of this world and, rather than offer Hope of Salvation and Eternal Happiness, they lead us further away from those Treasures. God wants us to Be Happy. He Created this world for us to care for and en-Joy. As our Wise Father, He KNOWS that false gods will ultimately lead to disappointment and pain, but He ALLOWS us to discover that for ourselves. ALLOW God's Presence within you to Be your Guiding Light, your Deepest Love, your Highest Truth.

Thou shalt not take the Name of The Lord, Thy God, in vain

Be Joyful when you speak or hear your Creator's Name... It is yours as well

There are many definitions for the word "vain". The first one in my dictionary says: "...Having no real value; Idle, Worthless...". Most people are quick to take offense if someone insults them or their family. Again, God does not want to prevent us from doing anything. He simply wants us to REMEMBER that we are His Children, carrying His Seed, The Christ Consciousness, within us. When I hear someone refer to God with Reverence and Love, I AM uplifted. If a person uses God's Name when they are angry or troubled, rather than being insulted, I say nothing and silently send them Love from my

Heart. We cannot help a person to REMEMBER their True Self by, as Beloved Mother Mary once shared, pointing fingers at them and pronouncing them guilty. As She also shared with me, "...We must Love our Brothers and Sisters into change...". When a person KNOWS Who he or she Really IS, then that person also KNOWS Who everyone else is ONE with.

Keep Holy the Sabbath — *Remember that...*
You are ONE with your Father

Back in the time of Moses, the Sabbath was the seventh day of the week, observed from Friday evening to Saturday evening, which was set aside as a day of rest and worship. In those days, the work was very hard, and the Sabbath was Truly a gift to man that he might rest, and worship his Father with others in the temple. In fact, until recently, it was against the law to sell alcohol before 2:00 pm on Sundays, and many stores were closed. Today, with the abolition of the "Blue Laws" and with most families having two wage earners, Sundays are treated like any other day (Remember the 60's movie "NEVER ON SUNDAY"?). People still go to their churches, temples and mosques, but they also do many other things, including "servile work". To repeat, God doesn't wish to prevent us from doing anything (..did He try to stop Eve from enjoying the apple? Everything is a choice...). When people ask me which church I belong to, I point to my Heart. I go to church 24/7, always trying to listen for God's Voice and BE AWARE of His Presence within me. Holy, to me, means Being WHOLE, or of ONE MIND with God. As I become more and more AWARE of God's Presence within me, I also get to behold Him everywhere "without" me. It is written in the BHAGAVAD GITA, which is the Hindu Holy Book: "...He who perceives me everywhere, and beholds everything in Me, never loses sight of Me, nor do I ever lose sight of him...". It is Truly a Joy to observe the events of my daily Life, and see myself as both the actor and the audience, with God Being the Loving Director.

Honor they father
and Thy mother

Acknowledge that God, your Creator...
Is your Wise and Powerful Father,
As well as your Loving, Nurturing Mother

God is Everything, Being both masculine energy, which is Wise and Powerful, and feminine energy, which is Loving and Nurturing. Symbols of those aspects of God are expressed through the Sun and the Moon. Being Created in God's Image, as extensions of Him/Her, we are Creations of Light Who are evolving into the AWARENESS of our True Identities. Some of us are Souls in male bodies, and others are Souls in female bodies, impersonating either a male or female. Our Destiny in this world is to manifest God, or The Christ Consciousness, through flesh and blood, as Beloved Master Jesus and other Ascended Souls, such as Lords Krishna and Buddha, did. To do that, we must PURIFY our minds and personalities of all false beliefs and limitations, and become totally balanced in all aspects of our Being...male, female and child. Jesus said we must be like "little children" to enter The Kingdom. Each of us is The Holy Family, which was symbolized by Jesus, Mary and Joseph. Our Earth parents did the best they knew to raise us and pass on what they learned from their parents. But, they could not Really teach us Who we were, because, in most cases, they didn't KNOW Who they were. In Truth, they are also Children of The One Parent and must also AWAKEN one day to their True Identities. This is God's Promise of Salvation.

Thou shalt not kill

Allow your brothers to Be
Who they are NOW...
And Revere all Life

God is Life. Therefore, everything that Lives is a Reflection of God. In the Koran, which is the Muslim Holy Book, the following passage expresses that idea: "...I was a Hidden Treasure and I wanted to Be KNOWN and so, I Created the world...". Trees, flowers, birds, animals, fish, insects, all Life reminds us of God...if we are open to it. Paramahansa Yogananda, the ONE-derful Indian Yogi who personified Love, once wrote: "...We see God in all Creation; in the rocks and minerals, God sleeps; in the flowers, God dreams; in the animals, God AWAKENS; and in man, God KNOWS He's AWAKE…". We as humans have the ONE-derful opportunity to become God-men…Divinity expressed through matter. God gave us free will to accomplish that end, and as much time as we require (Just like Bill Murray's character in "GROUNDHOG DAY"). The key to the whole adventure is the relinquishment of our little, separate wills, our ego's, and becoming ONE with God's Will by following Its Voice in our Hearts. The only commandments or conditions God gave us were to harm no one intentionally, and not try taking away another's free will. Doing so would be tantamount to "killing" their Spirits. Because we Live under the law of cause and effect, where we reap what we sow, we see so much suffering in this world. People are reaping the effects of past causes, or actions. There's a lot of Truth expressed in those 3 monkeys who see, hear and speak no evil, or the opposite of Love. Each of us can change our futures by changing our present actions. I KNOW this to Be a Truth, for I have seen it in my own Life experience. God ALLOWS us to Be who we are NOW…can we, as AWAKENING Children of Light, do less than that for our brothers and sisters?

Thou shalt not steal

Share God's Bounty…
For, all are ONE

In order for anything to flow freely, there can be no blockages. God's Bounty is in constant motion, flowing to and through everyone. When we block the flow through greed, fear of scarcity, or any other childish reason, we are denying God's Abundance and His Love for all of us. God's Treasure House is never empty, since we all dwell within It. Trying to steal or hoard is as silly (there's that inane ego again) as being locked up with another person in a room full of gold and jewels and attempting to hide or withhold some of the wealth. Beloved Lord Buddha once said: "…Speak the Truth; do not yield to anger; give, if asked. By these three you will become Divine…". I believe He understood the concept of Universal Bounty. Once we Realize that we are ONE and that God dwells within each of us, then we understand the teaching that when you give, you simultaneously receive. The gift is from God to God.

Thou shalt not commit adultery	*Strive to keep your Heart* *Pure... As It was Created*

As was discussed earlier, 3,000 years ago man was in a very carnal, darkened state and needed to be "controlled" until he was ready to be guided from within. We have reached the point where we are learning that we are totally responsible for everything that occurs in our Lives....we do, indeed, reap what we sow. (This sowing and reaping is also known as the law of "KARMA". My Beloved Master Merlin once described KARMA as simply a "lesson" that is experienced vs. being understood.) If 2 people wish to share their bodies with each other, then, SO BE IT. There can be no guilt associated with the action, if it was taken in each person's Truth and there was no intent to harm anyone. There are so-called "uncivilized" societies where sharing one's body freely with others is an integral part of their culture. Actually, because of their Innocence and Freedom, I believe these people are closer to their True Source than most people in the "civilized" world. We are Eternal Creations of Light. We are as God Created us, and in my understanding, adultery occurs when we taint or adulterate our Hearts with fear, which God did not Create, but which man made. When the Heart is Pure, only Good can spring from It. As Jesus once said: "...A Good tree cannot bring forth bad fruit...".

Thou shalt not bear false witness *Against thy neighbor*	*Stay in Integrity by always...* *Thinking, speaking and Living* *The Truth, as you understand it*

Integrity is consistency. Our actions do not belie our words, nor do our thoughts conflict with what we say and do. A person of Integrity is a Living example of his or her Truth. In this world, because the atrocities seem Real, and most people forget that THERE IS NO DEATH, it is difficult for them to understand that people such as Saddam Hussein are simply living out their own unique fantasy. To condemn him is to condemn your Self, for he is your Brother as surely as the other 5.5 billion Souls on this planet are. Not being in his mind or experiencing his innermost feelings, it is impossible to say what he is going through NOW. This much I do KNOW…when I AM Being True to my True Self, I AM in no pain, of any type, and am always Peaceful. When I AM experiencing pain, I must go within and ask God's Voice in my Heart to help me separate the Truth from the illusion, or, how am I not Being True to my Self, or God. Each of us must one day Speak, Live and BE God's Truth. When we accomplish that, we will have graduated from Earth's school and earned the right to move on. Thank You, Father.

Thou shalt not covet *Thy neighbor's wife*	*Know that you are complete…* *Through your Creator*

I feel that the previous discussions have explained both the Old and the New understandings which are written above. It is so very important to comprehend, until the time that we REAL-ize it, that there is nothing outside of God. Back in the 6th century, a wise and Loving entity once wrote:

> One is All; All are One. When you Realize this,
> What reason for holiness or wisdom?

I never cease to marvel at the Beautiful Simplicity of Truth!

Thou shalt not covet *Thy neighbor's goods*	*Realize that you always have* *What you need…NOW*

God Loves each of us and wants us to BE HAPPY. Being The Creator of "ALL THAT IS", He/She has everything to share with us. Being our Father, He will always look after us and ensure that our needs are met. If your earthly father were a billionaire, he could not even begin to give you What is already your inheritance and birthright, as a Child of God. BE Peaceful, establish your relationship with your Creator, and watch your Life change miraculously before your eyes.

Remember, everything down here is TEMPORARY….Beloved Lord Buddha understood the concept when He described a human lifetime as a "bubble in a stream" or "a flash in the night sky". This sojourn,

Soul Journey, on Earth is a mere nanosecond in Eternity....let's have FUN with it.!

One final thought: The Sufi's, who are the mystics of the Muslim religion, have a saying:

> *"First God is The Lover, and you are the Beloved,*
> *Then you are the Lover, and God is The Beloved.*
> *Finally, ALL is ONE."*

Let God Love you. He/She is waiting for Its wayward Children to come Home....

I Love You,
Michael

"HOW DO I PLAY?"

H *AVING GOOD FUN IS NOT A FINE ART,*
O *NE KNOWS HOW TO DO IT RIGHT FROM THE START,*
W *HEN WE WERE YOUNG BABES, WE AMUSED OURSELVES BY*

D *OWNLOADING THE LOVE WE RECEIVED FROM ON HIGH,*
O *UR JOY WAS COMPLETE FROM MORNING 'TIL NIGHT,*

I *N ALL SITUATIONS, WE WERE ONE WITH OUR LIGHT,*

P *ERHAPS NOW IT'S TIME FOR ME TO RETURN, TO A*
L *IFE THAT WAS SIMPLE, WITH NOTHING TO YEARN,*
A *ND ALL I NEED DO TO MAKE EACH DAY A JOY, IS SAY*
Y *ES! AND BE ONE WITH MY OWN LITTLE BOY*

Recently, during my walk through town (Seaside, Oregon), the conversations that I had with the various people I met along the way kept drifting toward playing and having fun. The previous day, I had gone to the "cove" after work. It's a place where one can sit in their car, en-Joy the incredible Beauty of the area and watch the waves end their journey with a splashy crash on the rocks at the water's edge. As I sat there savoring the show, I noticed a young Labrador Retriever swimming in the water, having the time of its Life. It was leaping through the surf like a gazelle, as Free as a dolphin.....I could sense its SHEER JOY in just PLAYING and BEING ALIVE.

At that moment, it occurred to me that I hadn't simply PLAYED in a long, long time. As with most of us, work and responsibility had completely overshadowed the INNER NEED to experience the JOY OF BEING ALIVE....the JOIE DE VIVRE that's always been missing from my Life. All work and no play has Truly made Mikey a dull boy. Six years ago, just before I was to leave for Tibet, Beloved Master Merlin stressed the importance of reconnecting with my own little boy. He described a process where I could sit quietly, close my eyes and call forth my inner child. That part of me could appear as a child, teenager or even a young man. When he showed up, I would then ask him what was his story....what was on his mind, and then, without judgment, help him to resolve the situation, whether it was conflict with another person, or just having some fun.

Although I did do some work in that area, I feel it's time, RIGHT NOW, to daily, hourly communicate with that part of me that desperately yearns to BE FREE AND JUST PLAY! SO BE IT!

6-05-1996

"SOME SOULFELT SMALLTALK"

S *AY "HOW ARE YOU", AND WHAT DO YOU HEAR?*
O *K FOR NOW, WHAT'S WITH YOU DEAR?*
M *Y NATURE'S TO CEASE RECITING THE LINES, TO*
E *XIT MY ROLE AND NOT REPLY: "FINE".*

S *O OFTEN MY HEART LONGS TO SING OF GOD'S*
O *NE-DER, AND MARVEL AT BOTH THE LIGHTNING AND THUNDER,*
U *NTIL I'M REMINDED I'D BE APT TO CAST PEARLS, TO BE*
L *OST IN THE QUAGMIRE OF THE OTHER PERSON'S WORLD.*
F *EELINGS ARE PART OF OUR GOD-CREATED SOULS, AND*
E *ACH ONE EX-PRESSED REMINDS US WE'RE WHOLE.*
L *OSE TOUCH WITH OUR EMOTIONS AND WE BREAK THE CONNECTION*
T *O GOD, OUR SELVES AND ALL THAT'S PERFECTION.*

S *OME MAY SURMISE THAT ALL THIS IS TOO HEAVY, AND*
M *AYBE THAT'S TRUE 'CAUSE THEY AREN'T QUITE READY. "BE*
A *LL THINGS TO ALL PEOPLE" WAS SOME SAGELY ADVICE*
L *EFT BEHIND LONG AGO BY MASTER JESUS, THE CHRIST.*
L *OVE WAS HIS MESSAGE 'TIL THE MOMENT HE "DIED",*
T *O FORGIVE AND LET LIVE AND REJOICE IN YOUR LIFE.*
A *LL FORMS ON THIS PLANET WILL PASS ON WITH TIME, BUT*
L *OVE AND ITS WORKS WILL ENDURE SO....BE*
K *IND*

7-04-1998

The above poem was written last Sunday, 6-28-1998, after a discussion between my Beloved Elspeth and me concerning our mutual discomfort with everyday “smalltalk”. We wondered how telephone conversations or meetings in the market might go if we eliminated the usual prattle and either spoke directly from our Hearts or just said nothing. Would the silence be deafening? So, my Beloved wrote a piece titled “SOULFULL SMALLTALK” and I proceeded to write “SOME SOULFELT SMALLTALK” vertically and see what my own Soul had to say about the matter. The resulting poem surprised me quite pleasantly because I hadn’t written anything in well over a year and it was GOOD to reconnect with that part of my Being and see that the connection was still very much intact.

My Dearest Friend and Mentor from “the other side”, Beloved Master Merlin, once presented me with a lesson where He stressed how important it was that we don’t allow ourselves to be “slimed” by others (interesting that the word “quagmire” appears in the poem). By this He meant that we should always use discernment when interacting with others and not say things that Truly would not be understood by those whose Hearts and minds were not quite as open as mine, possibly leaving myself open to labels such as kook, weirdo or some other such “slime”. Beloved Master Jesus gave similar advice 2,000 years ago when He cautioned: “…Cast ye not pearls before swine lest they be trampled upon….”. This was not a judgment against people but rather an observation that they weren’t ready to hear what was being offered.

Thus, treading the ridge between everyday talk about the weather and the ONE-derful Nature of thunder and lightning does, indeed, take the skill of a mountain goat. In either case, without getting too “heavy”, we can always send the person we are chatting with Love from our Hearts, by silently wishing them well and Sincerely being interested in them and what they have to say. For, we are all Children of God and it matters not where we are on the evolutionary ladder on Mother Earth. In The Creator’s Eyes, we are all equal….WE ARE ONE!

"WHAT IS A CHILD OF GOD?"

W *HOLE....NO MORE SPLIT MIND WITH A FEARFUL ego*
H *APPY....NO MORE HEAVY HEART, WEARING A "GRUMPY" MASK*
A *FFECTIONATE....NO MORE FEAR OF EX-PRESSING LOVE TO ALL*
T *RUSTING....NO MORE FEAR OF TAKING A STEP INTO THE UNKNOWN*

I *N-SPIRED....NO MORE LIVING FROM THEIR LOGICAL, egoic MIND*
S *AFE....NO MORE FEAR FOR THEIR PHYSICAL NEEDS OR PROTECTION*

A *BUNDANT....NO MORE BELIEF IN THEIR SCARCITY CONSCIOUSNESS*

C *HILD-LIKE...NO MORE PRETENSE AT BEING AN "IN CONTROL" ADULT*
H *ONEST....NO MORE FEAR OF EX-PRESSING THEIR TRUE FEELINGS*
I *NDESTRUCTIBLE....NO MORE FEAR OF SO-CALLED DEATH*
L *OVING....NO MORE EX-PRESSIONS OF ANY FORM OF FEAR*
D *EFENSELESS....NO MORE BELIEF IN ATTACK*

O *NE....NO MORE BELIEF IN SEPARATION*
F *REE....NO MORE IMPRISONMENT BY FEAR AND IGNORANCE*

G *UILTLESS....NO MORE BELIEF IN BEING A MISERABLE SINNER*
O *VERJOYED...NO MORE LACK OF THANKS FOR THE LIFE GIVEN THEM*
D *ESTINED....NO MORE DOUBT OF THEIR DIVINE PURPOSE*

7-04-1998

So many of us acknowledge that we are "Children of God", but really haven't a clue as to what that Truly means in our Lives. A good number of us are running around like confused, frightened children of some mean spirited, tight fisted, capricious human tyrant, who spends all of his time checking off the good and bad deeds we do, rather than en-Lightened Children of a Loving, Wise, All Powerful, All Knowing, All Giving Creator, or Divine Parent.

Because most of us take our existences for granted, the idea that each of us is actually a THOUGHT in GOD'S MIND that would disappear into nothingness, if God removed His/Her Attention from us for even an instant, is completely alien to us. The Depth of God's Unconditional Love for each and every ONE of Its Creations is unfathomable to our limited minds at this time. The fact that Hitler, Stalin and Pol Pot, to name just a few who were directly responsible for millions of deaths, were not instantly struck dead, gives us some idea of God's Unconditional Love and Divine Indifference towards us and what evil we do down here.

I don't believe that there is Divine Indifference concerning our AWAKENING and REMEMBERING our True Identities and, once again, BEING AS GOD CREATED US. As we fully REAL-ize our True Identity, all of our fears and limitations will just fade into nothingness like an early morning fog that's burned away by the Sun. A very Wise and Loving Teacher from the other side, Beloved Ramtha, once said that Freedom comes only to those who have faced, embraced and erased their limited selves, or ego's.

This is just another take on a very ancient theme. Beloved Lord Buddha said that Nirvana, or the final Liberation into Supreme Bliss, was reached when the ego was dissolved. Upon His achieving Enlightenment he said: "...Marvelous, marvelous, all mankind is already Enlightened, it is only their delusions which keep them from REAL-izing this...". On the same subject, He also said: "....When I achieved Enlightenment, I achieved absolutely nothing....".

Beloved Master Jesus encouraged us when He said: "....Be ye Perfect, even as your Father Which is in Heaven is Perfect..." and "...Know ye not that ye are Gods?...". Since He KNEW we were His Brethren, Children of God, Jesus KNEW that we had the same potential for Perfection that He demonstrated.

Buddha, Jesus and Krishna are only a few of the many Ascended Masters and Avatars Who have come to Earth trying to AWAKEN us to our TRUE IDENTITIES. With the millennium just around the corner, NOW is a Perfect time to reclaim our TRUE BIRTHRIGHT and all that it entails. With all the negativity and fear engulfing Beloved Mother Earth, our continued human existence depends upon it. SO BE IT!

"WHAT IS TRUE FREEDOM?"

W *ORRYING ABOUT NOTHING IS A GOOD START,*
H *AVING THE COURAGE TO ALWAYS FOLLOW ONE'S HEART,*
A *LLOWS US TO LIVE AS THE FREE SPIRITS WE ARE, STILL*
T *AKING THE TIME TO ENJOY LIFE'S BAZAAR*

I *NSTEAD OF GRAVE DOUBTS, OUR SOULS KNOW TO TRUST, AND*
S *URRENDER THEIR ego's TO THE INFINITE DUST*

T *HE TIME IS AT HAND WHEN LACK O' FAITH DISAPPEARS,*
R *EPLACING IT WITH TRUTH, BRIGHT, CRYSTAL AND CLEAR,*
U *NITING THE PARTS THAT MAKE EACH OF US WHOLE,*
E *TERNALLY, WE ARE SPIRITS, A.K.A. LOVING SOULS*

F *REEDOM WAS BESTOWED BY GOD ON EACH ONE, AND*
R *ETURNING AS LESS BELITTLES HER SONS,*
E *ACH TIME WE QUESTION WHETHER WE'RE TRULY FREE,*
E *NABLES OUR ego's TO CONTINUE TO BE*
D *IVINITY'S OUR NATURE,*
O *NLY WAITING TO BE FOUND, JUST*
M *AKE A SMALL EFFORT, AND YOUR SOUL WILL RESOUND!*

Shortly after my Beloved Elspeth and I arrived at my brother's vacation home in Vermont on 6-13-1998, we each wrote pieces on themes such as "SOULFELT SMALLTALK" and "WHAT IS A CHILD OF GOD?". Those writings were Created over the July 4th weekend, after which, the energy subsided for me, although I still felt there was another topic to write about....something to do with TRUE FREEDOM. We spent the summer working 3 days and PLAYING the other four. We planned to leave the area on August 20 and head out West, possibly settling in Santa Fe, NM.

On an afternoon a few days before we were to leave, my Beloved mentioned that she was going to finish writing her current piece, and then continue any future writings when we reached our new home.... wherever that may be. She asked me if I was going to write my piece about TRUE FREEDOM, and I said I didn't think so. However, while she started her "bathroom ritual", I wrote the words WHAT IS TRUE FREEDOM vertically and started to heed my Soul. By the time my Beloved was out of the shower, I had completed the above poem....with only one minor adjustment. It was quite a confirmation for me that I AND MY SELF WERE ONE...at that time! Of all the 100's of poems, etc. I've written over these past 11 years, the only other poem that was written as fast and as Purely was "IT'S A GREAT LIFE"...SO BE IT!

8-16-1998
(the 11th anniversary of The Harmonic Convergence...this is such Fun!)

"CELESTIAL TRINITY"

F *ROM WHENCE I FIRST CAME, ONLY I*
A *M IS CERTAIN,*
T *IS LIKE MY MEMORY'S BEEN*
H *ID BY A CURTAIN*
E *ACH DAY I A-*
R *ISE TO THE BRIGHT MORNING*

S *UN, AND GAZE*
U *P AT HIM KNOWING: I'M*
N *EVER JUST ONE*

M *Y SURENESS INCREASES AS I*
O *FFER MY HEART, AND*
T *ALK TO THE TREES WHO*
H *EAR MY REMARKS. THEY ARE THE OPE'*
E *ARS OF OUR DEAR MOTHER EARTH, THEY*
R *EMIND ME THAT SHE ALSO KNOWS*

E *ACH LIFE'S WORTH*
A *LL FORMS OF EXISTENCE,*
R *EGARDLESS OF SHAPE, ARE*
T *O THIS SWEET PLANET*
H *ER VERY OWN FACE*

A *T NIGHT WHEN THE HEAVENS ARE*
N *ATURALLY STARRY, I*
D *ISCOVER MY*

S *ISTER REFLECTING GOD'S GLORY*
I *NEVER GROW WEARY OF*
S *INGING MY PRAISES OF*
T *HE ONE WHO*
E *NLIVENS US WITH HIS*
R *ARE GRACES*

M *AY I ALWAYS REMEMBER THAT*
O *UR CELESTIAL TRINITY IS*
O *NLY A GLIMPSE OF GOD'S*
N *AME AND DIVINITY*

10-06-1999

"WHERE ARE YOU MY BELOVED SELF?"

W *HO WANTS TO KNOW WHERE I AM? I*
H *AVE ALWAYS BEEN HERE*
E *VEN IN YOUR DARKEST DAYS AND NIGHTS, I*
R *EMAINED CLOSE TO TOU*
E *VEN WHEN YOU HAVE*

A *SKED IF I EXIST, I*
R *EMAINED, LOVING YOU*
E *TERNALLY, I AM YOU,*

Y *OU ARE I. WE ARE*
O *NE*
U *NTIL TIME IS NO*

M *ORE,*
Y *OU WILL OFTEN FORGET THIS TRUTH*

B *E YOU, AND ALL*
E *LSE TRULY WILL NOT MATTER*
L *OVE YOUR CREATOR FIRST, AND*
O *NLY THAT ONE, FOR HE/SHE IS THE*
V *ERY FORCE THAT HAS GIVEN YOU*
E *TERNAL LIFE, A LIFE THAT CANNOT*
D *IE. THEN, LOVE ALL OTHERS, AS YOU LOVE YOUR SELF. THAT*

S *AID, RELAX AND*
E *NJOY YOUR*
L *IFE HERE ON EARTH. HAVE*
F *UN WITH IT, MY BELOVED MICHAEL*

10-07-1999

During the night of 10-6-1999, I kept hearing/seeing the words: WHERE ARE YOU MY BELOVED? The next night, actually early morning of 10-07-1999, during my sleep, the word SELF was added to the phrase. A few hours later, after my morning routine, I sat down and wrote the words vertically to see what my Soul, THE REAL I, wanted to say to my personality. In less than 10 minutes, the preceding was written...with no changes! Such a BEAUTIFUL, LOVING and LIBERATING message from my own TRUE SELF to my personality, which has been trying so hard these past 13 years to connect with the Soul....and deeper within the Soul, with the SPARK of DIVINITY, or CHRIST SELF.

Exactly 10 years ago, when I'd been experiencing a "DARK NIGHT OF THE SOUL", my Beloved Friend and Teacher, Beloved Master Merlin, assured me that, like a kernel of corn, THE SPARK was there, waiting for me to find it (During a different lesson, Beloved Master Merlin explained that God enlivens the Soul, and the Soul enlivens the personality....I later pictured the Triad of my Being as a spyglass with 3 sections in the 1 glass. I find it interesting that the more the glass is expanded, the further one can see. The first, or smallest section, by itself sees short distances, the third, or biggest section, together with the other 2, allows one to see the furthest.....personality....Soul....God. This sounds like a lesson in "Mind Expansion".).

I remember as a child, when trying to find something that was hidden by my parents, they would tell me if I was getting closer to the object of my search or further away by saying I was getting HOTTER or COLDER. I feel that, with this message, I am definitely getting HOTTER. SO BE IT!

“9-9-99”

N *OW*
I *S*
N *OW*
E *VERYWHERE*

N *OW*
I *S*
N *OW*
E *TERNALLY*

N *OW*
I *S A GLIMPSE OF*
N *ON-TIME AND*
E *TERNITY*
T *OMORROW IS A PROMISE,*
Y *ESTERDAY IS A MEMORY,*
N *OW*
I *S OUR*
N *ATURAL,*
E *TERNAL....STATE....ON EARTH*

On the very early morning of 9-9-99, a date that I’d been eagerly awaiting for quite a long time, I went outside and looked up at the billions of stars overhead and shouted to them: “...TODAY IS 9-9-99!...”....to which they replied: “...so?...”. The response I heard in my mind was somewhat disconcerting at first, but I soon REALIZED the Truth and went into the house and wrote the above ditty. Over these past 14 years, I’ve been reminded over and over again, in channelings, in numerous books and in countless philosophical tidbits passed down through the ages:....STAY IN THE PRESENT MOMENT. I remember even reading in a fortune cookie: “...We live in an eternity, the time to be happy is NOW...”. A dear friend was fond of saying: “...Yesterday is history, tomorrow is a mystery but, today is a gift, that’s why it’s called THE PRESENT....”.

Today is 9-10-2000, one year and a day since I penned my long anticipated ditty. It seems like I just wrote it the other day! Time is Truly losing its significance in my Life these days. I'm returning to work tomorrow after being out for 4 weeks, while I had shoulder surgery and recuperation time. During those 4 weeks, time seemed to be non-existent…the days were just a blur. My linear, time clock-controlled life was not a part of my current REALITY. I LOVED IT!

9-10-2000

PART IV

THE "CHRISTIE LIGHTHOUSE" CREATIONS

11-25-2002

Thru

11-25-2006

"AFFIRMATION OF UNITY"

I AFFIRM MY UNITY WITH MOTHER EARTH AND

THE BROTHERHOOD/SISTERHOOD OF HUMANITY,

AND I EXTEND THE HARMONY WHICH THEY REFLECT,

ONE PEOPLE, UNITED IN SPIRIT, INDIVISIBLE,

WITH PEACE, LOVE, TRUTH, FREEDOM AND

PROSPERITY FOR ALL GOD'S CREATIONS,

NOW AND FOREVER…..SO BE IT!!

Love, Michael

11-25-2002
(My 56th Birthday)

Back in the Spring of 1993, as my Beloved Elspeth and I were preparing for our first "LEAP OF FAITH" into the unknown, I was inSPIRED to paraphrase the American PLEDGE OF ALLEGIANCE into something more UNIVERSAL and UNITED. I wrote down the above AFFIRMATION OF UNITY on a small notepad and tucked it away until I acquired a word processor with which to type it in a finished format.

On 7-11-1993, we headed North up the 101/Pacific Coast Hwy and eventually settled in Cannon Beach, Oregon. Seven months later, we moved 8 miles north to Seaside where we stayed for the next 3½ years until the rain became so oppressive that we sold all of our belongings and moved to St. Thomas in the U.S. Virgin Islands. At that point, all of our worldly possessions were in 4 duffel bags. The St. Thomas experience was short lived, due to a number of factors that are discussed at great length in my "7 STEPS" work in progress, and we found ourselves moving back to New York City where I'd spent the first 30 years of my life. We stayed there for a year and then moved on to Vermont to spend the summer of 1998. Once again, we passed on or sold our furniture, etc. and were back to our 4 duffels. We left Vermont in August of 1998 and headed for the Southwest where we eventually settled in Durango, Colorado via Santa Fe, New Mexico. There were 4 moves in Durango, with the final one being our present (present = gift) home in Bayfield, Colorado......THE CHRISTIE LIGHTHOUSE.....a home that was built brand new, just for us, to our exact specifications, by ROCKY MOUNTAIN HOUSING which is owned by a DEAR CO-HEART named Greg.

After all that moving around, I was pleasantly surprised to find my little notebook tucked away with some other important papers. The above affirmation will always be my TRUTH, and it is my prayer that more and more of humanity will AWAKEN to the REALITY that, when you boil it down to gravy....WE ARE ONE.

"THE AWESOME POWER OF MIND EXPANSION"

T *AKING THE TIME TO*
H *EED OUR WISE HEARTS, IS AN*
E *XCELLENT MEANS OF*

A *PPROACHING THE START OF THE*
W *AY TO*
E *XPANDING THE MIND OF A*
S *OUL, BY*
O *PENING UP TO THE*
M *ERE*
E *ASE OF BEING WHOLE*

P *EOPLE HAVE LANGUISHED TOO LONG*
O *N THIS PLANE,*
W *EARING A MASK, ALWAYS TRYING TO*
E *XPLAIN.....THE*
R *EASONS WHY SUCH AND SUCH*

O *R THIS THING AND THAT*
F *IT INTO THE DOGMAS THAT*

M *AKE A MOCKERY OF THE FACT THAT*
I *N GOD'S IMAGE AND LIKENESS EACH*
N *TITY WAS CREATED, TO*
D *EMONSTRATE OUR DIVINITY, WHILE*

E *ARTHBOUND, BUT ELATED. BY*
X *PANDING ONE'S MIND WITH "WHAT IFS" AND*
P *ERHAPSES, WE ALLOW*
A *LL THOUGHTS TO REACH US WITHOUT ANY LAPSES.*
N *OW IS THE TIME TO*
S *AY ADIEU TO LIMITATIONS AND*
I *DENTIFY ONE'S SELF WITH*
O *UR NAMESAKE AND*
N *OT SEP'RATE NATIONS*

Love, Michael *1-16-2003*

During the last channeling that I was to have with Beloved Master Merlin, back in November of 1991, He spoke of making the shift from linear time to VERTICAL time. He described VERTICAL time as having 5 parts: the FIRST DIMENSION or ROOT, where all the archetypes of humanity's expressions dwelled. The roles of prince and pauper, hero and villain, beauty and the beast, ad infinitum all originated in the FIRST DIMENSION. The SECOND DIMENSION is the past of the current incarnation, as well as all lifetimes ever experienced. The memories of all the events of all lifetimes resided there. The THIRD DIMENSION is the present.....everything that's taking place NOW. Next comes the FOURTH DIMENSION which He described as REVELATION, which my dictionary describes as a STRIKING DISCLOSURE. After that was the FIFTH DIMENSION which He termed RESURRECTION, or A RISING FROM THE DEAD.

He explained that, while all 5 dimensions existed simultaneously, the 4th and 5th could only be reached through MIND EXPANSION. He didn't really elaborate on the term MIND EXPANSION, and it wasn't until many years later when I realized that, to me, it meant removing ALL LIMITING THOUGHTS from my belief system. I pictured the 5 dimensions existing at once as a huge, ancient redwood tree with deep, deep roots and branches that climb so high they couldn't be seen from the ground.

I recently went back and re-listened to earlier channelings with Beloved Master Merlin and I found that He <u>did</u> elaborate on MIND EXPANSION during those sessions. He would stress the importance of returning to a state of unlimitedness by activating one's pituitary gland, which increases the hormone flow to the pineal gland whereby the brain would receive unlimited thoughts which were just beyond social consciousness. He went on to explain that DESIRE was the means of getting the pituitary and pineal glands to AWAKEN dormant portions of the brain.....DESIRE to know The Father and become the Likeness of God. Loving one's Self enough to feel worthy to receive all that God is begins to bloom this little flower.....DESIRE to know that you and your Father are ONE. He continued that, when the pituitary is in full bloom, you cease to die or grow old, and the body is at your command.

After listening to those tapes, I was in-SPIRED to use the phrase "THE AWESOME POWER OF MIND EXPANSION" to create a poem, as I've been doing since "THE LAMPLIGHTER" writings which began in 1989. I've always been AMAZED at the intertwining of the poem and the narration that followed, or in some cases, preceded it. Now I understand that it all comes from THE RIVER OF THOUGHT which is THE MIND OF GOD. Many years ago, I wrote that each of us is a THOUGHT in THE MIND OF GOD WHO LOVES US SO MUCH that HE/SHE/IT allows us to do whatever we wish with nary a trace of judgment. Thus, the fact that we EXIST is the only proof we'll ever need that we are LOVED UNCONDITIONALLY by our CREATOR WITH WHOM WE ARE, INDEED, ONE.

It's very easy for me to see, NOW, that Beloved Master Jesus had expanded His mind to the fullest capacity for a human. His so-called miracles were, to me, COLLABORATIONS with THE FATHER within Him….."….I do these works not of myself but through the FATHER within me…". When He performed the TRANSFIGURATION of His body before a few of His disciples, we can see that He was simply raising His vibrations, reversing His body from density back into LIGHT. We know of His RESURRECTION which is the hope of humanity, for it demonstrated that THERE IS NO DEATH. No Soul ever perishes, but it is not necessary to experience physical death if we don't choose to. Jesus ASCENDED from this plane, taking His physical body with Him. He never wanted to be special, always insisting "…..greater works than these shall you do…", and "…..know ye not that ye are gods?…". He encouraged His listeners to aspire to their greatness when He said "….Be ye perfect even as your Father in heaven is perfect…". It appears that humanity has yet to grasp His message.

Following the 9-11-2001 bombings of the TWIN TOWERS in New York and the Pentagon in Washington, D.C., there was a wave of patriotism in the United States that swept the country almost to the point of hysteria. While understandable at a human level, it still saddened me to see that THE SEPARATION between peoples and nations was as wide as it's ever been. The ancient Romans said: "…if you want peace, prepare for war…". Now, today, the U.S. is preparing for war with Iraq and possibly North Korea. The book of REVELATIONS spoke of THE END DAYS being signaled by earthquakes, floods, WARS AND RUMORS OF WAR. So, if this was seen by our brother John in a vision 2,000 years ago……SO BE IT. I like our brother John (Lennon's) vision from 25 years ago in his song "IMAGINE". Here's an excerpt:

Imagine there's no countries
It isn't hard to do
Nothing to kill or die for
And no religion too
Imagine all the people
Living life in Peace
You may say that I'm a dreamer
But I'm not the only one
I hope someday you'll join us
And the world will live as one

Yesterday, January 15, was Martin Luther King Jr's birthday. He was slain, along with Gandhi, Lincoln and of course, Jesus, because some people didn't like what those Souls were saying. Because of Jesus' KNOWLEDGE that " …I AND MY FATHER ARE ONE….", He was able to "have the last laugh" by RESURRECTING His body, showing that sticks and stones may break His bones but, unlike HUMPTY DUMPTY, HE JUST PUT THEM BACK TOGETHER AGAIN!

My own PATH is CRYSTAL CLEAR……if Jesus, Buddha, Krishna, St. Germain and so many others with whom we're not familiar can expand their minds and KNOW that THEY WERE ONE WITH EVERYTHING, then,……..SO CAN I AND SO CAN YOU. All it takes is the DESIRE to do it and the ABSOLUTE LOVE of one's TRUE SELF. C'mon, let's GO FOR IT!

"PITY THE PERSONALITIES"

P *LAYING GAMES WITH PERSONALITIES*
I *SN'T SUCH FUN. IT'S FAR*
T *OO UNNATURAL WHEN*
Y *OU JUST SHUN AND SHUN*

T *O PEER BEYOND THE*
H *EAVY PERSONALITY MASKS, ENABLES*
E *ACH SOUL TO EMBRACE THEIR TRUE TASK*

P *EOPLE BEGIN TO FORGE THEIR FALSE FACE WHEN*
E *VER THEY ENTER THE UNIQUE HUMAN*
R *ACE. TOO*
S *OON THEY FORGET TO WHOM THEY*
O *WE THEIR REAL BEING, AND*
N *EVER REMEMBER THAT*
A *LL THIS IS QUITE FLEETING*
L *OVE ONE ANOTHER, EVEN*
I *F YOU CAN'T DO IT, 'CAUSE*
T *OGETHER, AS SIBLINGS,*
I *S THE*
E *ASY WAY THROUGH IT*
S *O BE IT!!*

Love, Michael

2-04-2003

More than a year ago, on the early morning of 1-28-2002, while waiting for my first customer at WAL*MART (I'm a cashier), I was thinking about something that Beloved Master Merlin shared with me many years ago. In reference to the human personality, He said: "....Take pity on the personality because it is the "garbage pail" of the mass consciousness' judgments, fears, beliefs, etc....". I wrote the words PITY THE PERSONALITIES vertically and, in less than 10 minutes, the above poem manifested.

From the day we are born into this world, we begin to forget our TRUE IDENTITY and start to create a false self, or personality (from the Latin persona, meaning mask) that takes the place of GOD, or our TRUE SELF. In most cases, the personality is taught only fear and limitation which is the opposite of its TRUE, SOUL NATURE of LOVE and FREEDOM. Although the personality never really buys into the whole idea, there is so much pressure from everyone they encounter to NOT BE WHO THEY ARE, that they find it's just easier to go with the flow than to resist it. By the time the personality realizes that it's been living a lie, pretending NOT TO BE rather than BEING WHO THEY REALLY ARE ONE WITH, the task of unraveling the twisted, knotted ball of twine that is their current life situation seems daunting and nearly impossible.

The one thing that makes the effort seem worth attempting is the possibility that the somewhat mediocre existence they've been living can be replaced by THE TRUTH of Who they TRULY ARE ONE WITH.......the struggling, lowly, dust covered caterpillar emerges as the BEAUTIFUL, FLIGHTFUL BUTTERFLY! I like to envision the personality as the glass chimney on an oil lamp, or the glass door of a wood stove. The personality must be shiny, sparkly for the world to fully enjoy the lamp or the stove.......our job is to cleanse the personality of all its negativity so that the FLAME WITHIN MAY BE SEEN AND ENJOYED. By removing, or cleansing, the parts of our BEING that are not WHO WE TRULY ARE, we allow THE TRUE SELF to be REVEALED. When someone complimented Michelangelo on his latest sculpting masterpiece (THE PIETA, DAVID?), the artist replied that the creation was always there in the block of marble, he just chipped away the small pieces!

The previous paragraphs pretty well summed up my situation 16 years ago, on my fortieth birthday. I've been unraveling my ball of twine, chipping away the small pieces since then, as is being recorded in my "7 STEPS" work in progress, and I'm here to tell you that IT TAKES WORK, but it's worth it! My recent work: "THE AWESOME POWER OF MIND EXPANSION" is testament to that fact. Living day to day as a FREE, GOD-CENTERED SOUL rather than a frightened personality, while oftentimes alienating, is incredibly REFRESHING, like standing at the seashore on a bright, breezy day. The alienation (alien-nation) comes from BEING "temporarily" different from most others because of an alternate belief system, or modus vivendi (way of living).

Yesterday, February 3, 2003, I felt extremely ENERGIZED, as if my body had raised its vibrations a notch. That feeling allowed me to treat the 200 or so customers I encountered, no matter what type of behavior they were presenting to me, with more COMPASSION, FORBEARANCE (self control) and TOLERANCE than I had to that point. IT FELT GREAT!! More than 16 years ago, Beloved Master Merlin advised me:"....You're not responsible for others' responses to you....they must take credit for what they are, too....". I've grappled with that bit of advice for all these years, but yesterday, for the first time, I didn't allow anyone to GET MY GOAT, or, in other words, DISTURB MY PEACE. Rather than "SHUT DOWN" when a person didn't respond to my greeting, I simply smiled to myself and sent them LOVE. WHAT'S NOT TO LIKE ABOUT THAT?!

When I, and each of us can say with GREATEST SINCERITY and CONVICTION: "....I AM GOD, AND ALL THAT I SEE DO I LOVE.... FOR I AM ALL I SEE....AND I LOVE WHAT I AM...", we will have arrived at HEAVEN ON EARTH. SO BE IT!

"BEGINNING TO RECOGNIZE UNLIMITED THOUGHTS"

After finishing my "THE AWESOME POWER OF MIND EXPANSION" poem and essay on 1-16-2003, I began asking my OWN TRUE SELF/LORD GOD OF MY BEING/SOUL to start sending me UNLIMITED thoughts so that I might continue to EXPAND MY MIND and begin using and ENLIGHTENING the dormant parts of my physical brain that are just waiting to be activated and filled with LIGHT. This process will eventually lead to the infusing of every cell of my body with LIGHT, thus moving from a gross, dense physical body to a finer, LIGHTER one. This PATH is the only one that makes any sense to me since, in all my 56 years on the planet, nothing else has really interested me. To BECOME the LIVING GOD EXPRESSED (pressed out) through my flesh and blood is to BECOME THE CHRIST OF GOD......THE SON of THE HOLY TRINITY:....FATHER (CREATOR or SOURCE), SON (CHRIST CONSCIOUSNESS in a physical body), HOLY (WHOLE-I) SPIRIT (That aspect of GOD WHO KNOWS THE TRUTH, yet perceives the illusions of this world).

This path is not one of self aggrandizement (to make me greater, more powerful or special), but rather to attain the level of human perfection that Beloved Master Jesus said we all could attain. If a Soul such as I who lived a so-called normal existence, with nothing remarkable to say about what's transpired so far, can reach the HIGHEST LEVEL OF HUMAN EXPRESSION as Jesus, Buddha, Krishna and a host of others have, then, SO CAN WE ALL. This is THE HOPE OF THE WORLD, and I believe with ALL MY HEART that there are thousands like me RIGHT NOW who are WORKING towards the same end. At this time, the world is probably at the darkest point in its modern history.....wars, threats of wars, unrest and injustice in every corner of the globe, people starving to death by the thousands daily, unbridled greed, separation from each other and MOTHER EARTH, falsity in business, politics and religion on a scale never before witnessed....the litany can go on and on but, IT'S ALWAYS DARKEST BEFORE THE DAWN.....and I believe this time will lead those of us who remain after the PURIFICATION PERIOD to the GOLDEN DAWN OF THE NEW AGE!

Love, Michael

2-11-2003

Getting back to the title of this work, these past couple of days have brought some very exciting thoughts and REVELATIONS to me. I'll list them below with an accompanying narration if inspired:

- *2-7-2003 Commented to my Beloved Elspeth that, for the first time in my life, I didn't wish to leave the planet. I didn't want to be "beamed up" but rather wanted to stay because of the EXCITEMENT I was feeling as world events seemed to be progressing (retrogressing?) at an accelerated rate. I felt that THINGS WERE STARTING TO HAPPEN and that people were going to need/heed whatever words of LOVE and WISDOM I had to share with them, as well as being in-SPIRED by my SUPER DUPER example of a Soul living in a body. I like to use the example of a balloon that needs the AIR (SPIRIT) to fill the plastic container (body). Just as a HUMAN needs the Soul and the body to BE A HUMAN, the balloon needs the air and the receptacle to BE A BALLOON.*

- *2-10-2003 The thought occurred to me that my biological father who passed away on 2-16-2001 had reincarnated and was back on the planet as a toddler. This thought was so powerful that I felt my body begin to QUICKEN to such a point that my breathing began to become rapid.*

- *2-10-2003 Right after the previous thought, another one came suggesting that, even if he/she (the Soul) didn't recognize me, I WOULD RECOGNIZE HIM/HER. At this point, my breathing became so rapid that I was breathless and exhausted. I can't remember the last time I felt this way just from THOUGHTS. I was reminded of beloved Master Merlin's words when He said that I would be able to tap into my SOUL MEMORY but that it would take many mental adjustments. SO BE IT!*

"OUR BLINDFOLDED JOURNEY"

O *N THE DAY OF OUR BIRTH, A VEIL IS*
U *NFURLED TO KEEP US FROM GETTING A*
R *EAL VIEW OF THE WORLD*

B *LINDED, WE STUMBLE AND GROPE THROUGH THIS*
L *IFE, FORGETTING THAT TRUTH DWELLS*
I *NSIDE, 'MIDST THE STRIFE*
N *EVER IS OUR*
D *IVINITY FAINTLY*
F *AR FROM OUR selves, ALTHOUGH*
O *UR ego's WHINE THAT, GOD'S*
L *EFT US IN HELL*
D *ESPITE its VAIN SCREECHING, OUR*
E *go's RUSE IS REVEALED, AND THE*
D *AY IS APPROACHING, WHEN WE'LL BE FULLY HEALED*

J *UST LIKE A BLIND PERSON, PLEASE RELY*
O *N YOUR GUIDE, AND LET IT EXPLAIN WHY*
U *SEEM TO BE WITHOUT SIGHT. IT'S A TEST TO*
R *ETURN US TO OUR TRUE,*
N *ATURAL SOURCE, AS WE ALWAYS PAY HEED TO ITS*
E *TERN' AND*
Y *'S INNER VOICE*

Love, Michael
8-24-2004

I was inspired to write the above poem nearly a month ago, after a brief conversation with someone at work (WAL-MART demo lady Daisy). We were discussing how everyone seems to be walking in their sleep and groping here and there, not really conscious of where they were or what they were doing. During that chat, I was reminded of something I'd read many years ago where the entity (a Spirit Guide named WHITE FEATHER) described the Soul's journey through LIFE as being a blindfolded one, and that a person must just ".....keep on keeping on....." and TRUST that the final outcome was CERTAIN. That remembrance sparked an idea and I shared with "Miss Daisy" that I felt the way a person could remove the blindfold was to recognize the VOICE OF THEIR HEART and then follow it UNCONDITIONALLY. She tended to agree.

Since my fortieth birthday nearly 18 years ago, I've been writing up a storm, with the basic theme always seeming to be about following one's HEART, or heeding the VOICE FOR GOD within you. We each have 2 voices; the first is the voice of our conscious minds, the ego, where everything it knows and believes is based upon its past and the teachings of others......of course, most people's pasts are filled with numerous painful, fear-filled experiences which, if not dealt with and LOVINGLY released, will virtually paralyze a person and prevent them from discovering their TRUE POWER. The ego's voice is usually chattering non stop and is filled with negativity, doubt, guilt, lack of FAITH and, of course, fear. The second VOICE, the VOICE FOR GOD, sometimes referred to as ".....the still, small VOICE....." can only be Truly heard when the ego's voice, the chatterbox, is stilled. This can easily be accomplished by meditating, which can be as simple as sitting in a quiet place, (it needn't involve ritualistic AUMing or staring at a candle's flame), listening to your breathing and then responding to what you hear when your mind is quiet (this is the TRUE meaning of responsibility or RESPONSE-ability). Unlike the ego's screeching voice, the VOICE of our HEARTS is soothingly PEACEFUL and is always POSITIVE, CERTAIN, NON-JUDGMENTAL, TRUSTING and, of course, LOVING....a very easy VOICE to recognize, once you quiet the magpie-like ego's tiny mouthpiece. I used to liken the 2 voices to the old cartoons' depictions of a character having a devil on one shoulder and an angel on the other (how perceptive those people were).

Shortly after my fortieth birthday, which was 11-25-1986, I wrote something on 12-02-1986 which I titled: "MY TRUTH". Here it is :

IF THE STILL, SMALL VOICE FOR GOD WITHIN YOU
SUGGESTS THAT YOU DO SOMETHING,
AND YOU CHOOSE TO DO IT,
THEN BY DOING IT,
YOU TURN UP THE VOLUME OF THAT VOICE,
AND MOVE CLOSER TO BECOMING THAT VOICE

That ONE-derful VOICE is our own HEAVENLY "guide dog" that will HAPPILY help us negotiate this "blindfolded journey". There have been so many instances during these past seventeen plus years where I followed my HEART unconditionally and was always rewarded, whether I observed the results of my actions or not. On the other hand, there were times when I didn't heed the "still, small VOICE" and I was filled with regret. Of course, those were simply learning experiences to help me reach the point where I would always FOLLOW MY HEART UNCONDITIONALLY and UNERRINGLY.....which, I am HAPPY to say, I DO!!

This LIFE that GOD gave us is really quite simple......once you take the ego out of the equation and put it in its proper place. As I used to share with my children when they were growing up: ".....money is a wonderful servant, but a terrible master....". The same can be said of the ego. GOD BLESS US, EVERYONE!

"DEATH IS ONLY AN OPTION"

D *YING, THEY SAY, IS THE OTHER CERTAINTY, PUTTING AN*
E *ND TO MOST SOULS' MISERY*
A *SCENSION IS RESERVED FOR SAINTS AND AVATARS,*
T *OO LOFTY FOR THOSE BENEATH THE BRIGHT STARS*
H *OW DID THIS STRANGE THEORY EVER COME TO TAKE ROOT?*

I *S DEATH, AS THEY SAY, THE ULTIMATE TRUTH?*
S *OMETHING INSIDE ME PURRS: " CONSIDER PLAN B*

O *R YOU'LL JUST KEEP ON DYING THROUGHOUT ETERNITY "*
N *OW IS THE TIME TO CHOOSE LIBERATION, AND*
L *IVE YOUR SWEET LIFE LIKE A GREAT CELEBRATION*
Y *OU ONLY LIVE ONCE IS A STATEMENT OF FACT*

A *ND WITHIN THAT ONE LIFE IS A MYRIAD OF ACTS*
N *EVER DO WE LOSE OUR CONSTANT STATE OF MIND*

O *R NEED TO SURRENDER THE HOME WHERE WE RESIDE*
P *ITUITARY AND PINEAL ARE THE GLANDS TO INFINITY, AND*
T *AKING THE BODY TO "HEAVEN" IS ACCOMPLISHED QUITE EASILY*
I *T INVOLVES MIND EXPANSION AND RELEASE OF LIMITATION, TO*
O *PEN ONE'S SELF TO GOD'S GLORIOUS IMAGI-*
N *ATION*

Love, Michael

2-09-2005

Some of us have heard that Jesus, Mary, Saint Germain, Baba Ji and many, many others with whom we are unfamiliar have taken their bodies with them to other dimensions, or planes, and returned to Earth looking as they did when they left. Although the idea of taking one's body with them may seem farfetched, that "farfetchedness" is a judgment that will keep us from receiving unlimited or "unaltered" thoughts.

Ever since I was a young boy, I always believed that, no matter what thought came to me, no matter how seemingly impossible it may be, somewhere in God's OMNIVERSE that thought was a REALITY. We can just look at the last 100 years of humanity's history to see that what was once just an idea or a dream, such as air travel, space travel, radio, television, etc., etc., became a manifested REALITY, although the technology to do those things was, like GOLD, always there, waiting to be discovered. The ideas all come from GOD'S MIND, or THE UNIVERSAL RIVER OF THOUGHT, and the more we allow ourselves to welcome new thoughts into our minds, without altering them with judgments of good or bad, possible or impossible, right or wrong.......these judgments come from our "altered" ego which only accepts what it is familiar with and has experienced, thus "altering" the new thought and sending it back to God.....the more of these unlimited thoughts we will receive.

In my work "THE AWESOME POWER OF MIND EXPANSION", which was created on 1-16-2003, I discuss the activation of the pituitary and pineal glands by DESIRING to KNOW THE CREATOR and become the LIKENESS OF GOD. By DESIRING to know that "I AND MY FATHER ARE ONE", we begin to bloom the ONE-drous flower of the pituitary, and thereby increase its hormone flow to the pineal which activates dormant portions of our brains. The more receptive we are, the more we will receive. When the pituitary is in full bloom, we cease to die, we cease to grow old, and whatever we tell the body to do, it will do.........including ASCENDING into another dimension. If I have the thought, then somewhere it is already SO. I believe with all my HEART that ASCENSION is one of the "perks" of BEING a SOUL in a physical body.

Rod Serling, the creator of "THE TWILIGHT ZONE", once gave his definition of SCIENCE FICTION and FANTASY. He said: "…..Science Fiction takes the improbable and makes it possible; Fantasy takes the impossible and makes it probable….". Certainly Mr. Serling was a visionary, as so many of his " TWILIGHT ZONE" episodes attest, but, perhaps he was also limited by HIS altered ego which judged what was possible and what wasn't.

Many of us LIGHT workers are also PIONEERS who are blazing a path into the unknown, or as Gene Roddenberry, the creator of "STAR TREK" would say: "…….going where no human has gone before…". My opening comment about Jesus, Mary, etc. belies that statement, but certainly no one in modern times, not even Paramahansa Yogananda, whose SOUL consciously left his body, has demonstrated ASCENSION to the world.

We live in an ETERNITY, let's move beyond the "monkey minds" of social consciousness and show the world some of the extraordinary gifts that were bestowed by GOD on HIS/HER/ITS Children. It will make the "moon landing" look like a walk in the park, and help usher in THE GOLDEN AGE of PEACE, LOVE, TRUTH and INNOCENCE that MOTHER EARTH and all HER inhabitants so richly deserve. As Jackie Gleason used to say after the June Taylor Dancers did their thing and he was getting ready to do one of his famous skits: "…….AND AWAAAAAY WE GO!……"

"I AM MY OWN MIDDLE MAN, AS ARE YOU"

I *S THE SMALL VOICE INSIDE YOU*

A *SKING FOR YOUR ATTENTION?*
M *AYBE YOU CAN'T HEAR IT 'CAUSE THERE'S TOO*

M *UCH CONTENTION , 'TWEEN*
Y *OUR SELF AND YOUR ego, SO YOU*

O *NLY HEAR CHATTER, PERHAPS NOW'S THE TIME TO ASK:*
W *HAT REALLY MATTERS? IT'S*
N *EVER TOO LATE TO*

M *AKE YOUR CONNECTION WITH THE*
I *AM INSIDE YOU; THAT'S*
D *IVINE INTERVENTION. THERE'S NO NEED TO*
D *ISCOVER A GURU OR*
L *AMA, 'CAUSE WE WERE CREATED WITH THE GREAT*
E *SCAPE FROM THE DRAMA*

M *AN'S SOUL IS DIRECTLY CONNECTED TO GOD*
A *ND TUNING RIGHT IN TO IT IS*
N *OT VERY HARD*

A *LL THAT'S REQUIRED IS A*
S *TRONG, HEARTFELT DESIRE TO*

A *LLY ONESELF WITH THE HEAVENLY FIRE, BY WANTING TO*
R *EMEMBER THE TRUTH OF YOUR B-*
E *ING, AND WISHING TO KNOW*

Y *OUR REAL IDENTITY*
O *NCE YOU DO THAT, IT'S EASY AS PIE TO SOAR UP, UP AND*
U *P TO YOUR HOME IN THE SKY*

Love, Michael *2-15-2005*

The other day at work, during my afternoon break, I kept getting the thought: "I AM THE MIDDLEMAN", and VOILA! the poem on the previous page was Created a few days later. The poem talks about not needing a guru or lama to remember Who we are, because we were Created with everything required to REMEMBER GOD. The word RELIGION comes from the Latin RELIGARE, meaning to reconnect, but as we can see, religion has pretty much failed in its job of reconnecting the SOULS OF HUMANITY back to GOD. As I've mentioned in earlier pieces, my Beloved Friend and Mentor, Merlin the ONE-drous Wizard, used to say that: ".....GOD enlivens the SOUL, and the SOUL enlivens the personality....". Once again, it all goes back to GOD. When referring to the word GURU, a sweet lady named Krystiahn used to say: " .....GEE, YOU ARE YOU!.....". Jesus advised His disciples not to look outside themselves, but rather to seek THE KINGDOM OF HEAVEN, or GOD, That was within their own SOULS.

For more than 18 years, I've been writing poems and essays dealing with "THE AWAKENING", or remembering our TRUE SELVES, or SOULS. Once we do that, I believe, GOD will take the final step for us as we also REMEMBER HIM/HER/IT and fall BLISSFULLY IN LOVE WITH OUR OWN CREATOR. As I've shared earlier, Paramahansa Yogananda, the great Indian mystic and saint, once said: "......We see GOD in all creation; in the rocks and minerals......GOD SLEEPS; in the flowers......GOD DREAMS; in the animals......GOD AWAKENS; and in man......GOD KNOWS HE'S AWAKE.....".

To me, the implication of the last statement is that in AWAKENED MAN we have GOD in full expression. To become a CHRIST is TO BE GOD expressed in flesh and blood. When Jesus proclaimed that ".....I AND MY FATHER ARE ONE...", was He being schizophrenic, or was He stating a simple TRUTH? Paramahansa understood the concept when he referred to humanity as "SOUL WAVES" on the SEA OF GOD'S SPIRIT. The wave is not the ocean, but it is ONE WITH THE OCEAN and it contains all the qualities of the ocean.

William Blake (1757-1827), the English visionary and poet, was considered insane during his lifetime. He once said to a houseguest that:"....I cannot think of death as more than the going out of one room into another....". When his guest put the popular question to Blake concerning the DIVINITY of Jesus, Blake replied: "...He is the only GOD...." but then he added "...And so am I and so are you...". Blake KNEW Who he was, and he KNEW Who everyone else was....... INFINITE EXPRESSIONS OF THE ONE SOURCE. It's been said that no two snowflakes are alike and that no two grains of sand are alike either. This latter fact really impressed me, since theoretically, it could be verified, and I asked a very conservative gentleman I know, who happens to be a geologist, if it were true. His response to me was: "..... There may be 2 alike.....". If something as simple as sand can have such an infinite number of expressions, why is it so difficult for humans to accept that each of them is a UNIQUE EXPRESSION OF GOD?

The answer, I believe, lies in the un-TRUTHS that have been instilled in man as far back as can be recorded. Whatever the reason for them; control, ignorance, cowardice, laziness, unworthiness, etc., etc., I believe that NOW is the time for the Souls of humanity to REMEMBER WHO THEY TRULY ARE, and get on with the business of CREATING HEAVEN ON EARTH........which is why we were put here in the first place.....eons ago. We were created by LOVE, to LOVE...... LOVE IS OUR SOUL PURPOSE. My most recent writing before this one ," DEATH IS ONLY AN OPTION", talks about expanding our minds to the point that we need never leave our bodies.....unless we choose to. We can raise the vibrations of the body we are inhabiting so high that, like a fan on maximum speed, it would seem to disappear and, as Blake said, just go from "room" (plane) to "room" (Jesus said: ".....In my Father's house there are many mansions....").

My Beloved Brothers and Sisters, we are all like the struggling caterpillar who has no idea of the GLORIOUS LIFE that's ahead......... or does it? As the poem explains, once we have the DESIRE TO REMEMBER WHO WE ARE, the rest is as easy as pie.....GOD IS WAITING FOR US TO ASK.

"WE ARE BRANCHES ON THE VINE"

W *HEN WILL WE REALIZE THAT*
E *VERYTHING AND EVERYONE*

A *LL*
R *CONNECTED TO*
E *ACH OTHER*

B *Y THE MOST*
R *ADIANT AND*
A *WE INSPIRING*
N *ERGY, KNOWN AS*
C *REATION, OR GOD, OR THE UNIVERSE, THAT*
H *AS ALWAYS AND WILL ALWAYS*
E *XIST BEYOND OUR*
S *IMPLE AND VERY LIMITED COMPREHENSION?*

O *UR REALIZATION OF THAT TRUTH WILL*
N *D THE DEEP SOUL SLEEP*

T *HAT*
H *AS KEPT US SEPARATED FROM*
E *ACH OTHER AND ALL THINGS. GOD IS THE*

V *INE, AND WE ALL ARE*
I *NDIVIDUAL BRANCHES THAT ARE "DA"-VINE, TOO*
N *OW IS THE TIME TO REMEMBER OUR*
E *TERNALLY BRILLIANT AND GLORIOUS SELVES!*

Love, Michael

7-27-2005

One of my favorite quotes, already cited earlier, states:

*"One is all; all
are one. When you realize this,
what reason for holiness or wisdom?"*

How does one achieve this state of KNOWING THE TRUTH? Beloved Master Merlin once stated that "…..DESIRE is the ticket to Paradise. To become a Christ is to DESIRE to KNOW the Father and become the likeness of GOD…..". To this day, I still share with anyone who is so kind to ask what I'm "waiting for" that, I want to remember GOD consciously, that is, in my physical organ known as the brain (I already KNOW Him/Her/It in my Heart). I feel that once I consciously remember WHOM I AM ONE WITH, this human drama will be complete for me. That is not to say that I'll be leaving the planet, but rather I'll be able to help others who are searching for the TRUTH, to find it.

In the Buddhist tradition, their term for Beings who have attained ENLIGHTENMENT, or freedom from darkness and illusions, and are entitled to move on to NIRVANA, but choose to stay behind to help others achieve liberation, is "BODDHISATTVA". They offer a parable to explain the concept:

"….A group of travelers has been walking through the scorching desert for weeks. Exhausted and dehydrated, they come to a high wall in the middle of nowhere. The leader of the group climbs the wall and to his amazement and delight he finds an oasis of indescribable beauty on the other side. Fountains, fruit trees, waterfalls and fragrant flowers are just a few of the wonders he beholds. As he climbs down to the other side, the next person climbs up and does the same thing. One by one they follow suit until one of the men climbs up, looks around, climbs down to his weary friends and begins walking back into the desert. A companion asks him why he didn't go over the wall and where was he going. His reply was: "……I'm going back to help others find this HEAVENLY place…".

My beloved brothers and sisters, we ARE all in this together. I, for one, am TRULY tired of the daily drama and, with all my HEART, DESIRE TO REMEMBER THE TRUTH OF MY BEING (Since I began this journey nearly 20 years ago, I've felt that we all were suffering from amnesia, and that this time in humanity's evolution was to BE the time of AWAKENING). When I do, it will be my supreme PLEASURE and PRIVILEGE to share how I got there with others who've had enough of this game. We were sent here eons ago to be caretakers of the planet. Mother Earth is patiently waiting for us to remember that TRUTH and begin the next chapter of our ETERNAL Lives. SO BE IT!

"WE ARE ALL WORKS IN PROGRESS?"

W *HAT IS THE PURPOSE OF*
E *VOLUTION? IF WE WERE*

A *LL CREATED FROM GOD'S SUBSTANCE,*
R *WE NOT ALREADY AS PERFECT AS GOD? IS*
E *VOLUTION JUST AN ELABORATE GAME TO*

A *LLOW THE SOULS OF CREATION TO*
L *IVE AND EXPERIENCE THE COUNTLESS*
L *EVELS OF AWARENESS THAT*

W *E ALREADY KNOW BUT, LIKE AN*
O *FTEN WATCHED FAVORITE MOVIE, ENJOY*
R *EVIEWING AND EXPERIENCING OVER AND OVER?*
K *NOW THY "SELF" IS A*
S *AYING FROM ANCIENT GREECE;*

I *F WE TRULY KNOW WHO WE ARE, THEN*
N *OTHING CAN DISTURB OUR*

P *EACE OR*
R *EPLACE OUR ESSENCE, WHICH IS GOD. IN THE*
O *RIENTAL LAND OF INDIA, LIFE'S COMEDY/DRAMA IS CALLED "LILA", OR*
G *OD'S "SPORTIVE PLAY".*
R *ETURNING TO OUR SOURCE IS AS*
E *ASY AS*
S *AYING THAT THE GAME IS OVER AND OUR*
S *OUL PURPOSE IS LOVE.*

Love, Michael

10-19-2005

In my introduction to "THE LAMPLIGHTER", which was first put together on March 26, 1990, I list some quotes from Matthew's Gospel which was his own unique experience of Jesus and His teachings. One of the quotes I used was:

> *"...Be ye therefore perfect, even as your Father Which is in Heaven is Perfect..."*
>
> *Matthew 5:48*

In referring to that quote in my introduction, I suggested that Jesus was stating a TRUTH and that He was encouraging each of us to live up to and ex-PRESS our TRUE potential. Because so many of us identify with our body/personalities, we have forgotten WHO WE TRULY ARE. It's like an actor portraying a villain, hero, victim or some other character getting so caught up in their role that they forget who they really are. That's about as simple an analogy that I can offer.

In order for us to return to a GOD-centered consciousness, we must change our minds about who we are. The ego/personality-centered consciousness believes in separation, sickness, old age and death. The SOUL/GOD-centered consciousness KNOWS that the opposite...... UNITY, HEALTH, ETERNAL YOUTH and ETERNAL LIFE.....are the TRUTH of our BEING. Each morning, during my shower, I say ALOUD the following to call forth my SOUL:

".....I AM THE SOUL; I AM THE LIGHT DIVINE; I AM LOVE;

I AM (GOD'S) WILL; I AM FIXED DESIGN (I have a DESTINY)....."

Working as a cashier at WAL-MART, I get to wait on 800-1,000 people each week. When a customer comes up and asks me how I am, I reply: ".....SUPER DUPER, how are you?....". The responses I receive vary from " I THINK I'M GONNA MAKE IT" and "HANGIN' IN THERE" to " I'M NOT SUPER DUPER BUT I'M OK" and, sometimes "ME TOO". I encourage the latter group to speak the words and ZAP me with their positive energy. I explain that it's like telling someone you LOVE them and their response is "ditto" or "me too", rather than their saying I LOVE YOU TOO!

When I put together my first book of poetry in 1988, "BABYSTEPS", I subtitled it : " The early poetry of one man's AWAKENING". Next month, on November 25, 2005, will mark the 19th anniversary of my 40th birthday and my first meeting with Beloved Master Merlin. With the exception of a few stumblings along the way, I have never wavered from my PASSIONATE desire of REMEMBERING WHO I AM and then sharing my experience with others who also want to REMEMBER (I haven't met any as yet). Oftentimes I share with my Beloved Elspeth that I have put all my eggs in one basket.....THE AWAKENING. With all my HEART, I believe that the way things are now......separation, greed, lack of courtesy, war, starvation, deprivation, etc., etc......is coming to an end. I always share with people that I see a big, RED STOPLIGHT that will be THE CREATOR's way of saying: ".......playtime is over; it's time to AWAKEN AND BE THE CHILDREN OF GOD AGAIN.....".

I believe that I will see that RED LIGHT before my time on Mother Earth is up. If I'm mistaken, then oh well, "....c'est la vie....", and that's life. I wouldn't have had these past 19 years any other way. When Siddartha Gautama, who was later to become the BUDDHA, confronted His father, the king, and questioned why He had been sheltered from seeing the ravages of sickness, old age and death, His father replied that all of humanity lived under that curse and he didn't want his son to be troubled by it (when Siddartha was born, prophet's said He would either be a great king or a great teacher.....guess what His father was pulling strings for). Siddartha's reply was: "......I will lift this curse of sickness, old age and death from the shoulders of mankind.....that is my DESTINY.....". When the BUDDHA had His AWAKENING under the BODHI tree, He KNEW the TRUTH of his BEING and, as Beloved Master Jesus said 500 years later, IT set Him FREE. SO BE IT!

"THE BLESSINGS OF WAITING"

T *RYING TO MAKE THINGS*
H *APPEN, RATHER THAN ALLOWING*
E *VERYTHING TO MATURE IN ITS PROPER TIME,*

B *EGETS A DISTINCTIVE*
L *ACK OF INNER PEACE THAT*
E *NSURES THE CREATION OF*
S *TORMS IN OUR PSYCHE, THAT*
S *HOW THE OUTSIDE WORLD WHAT OUR*
I *NNER WORLD IS LIKE AT THE MOMENT.*
N *OW, ALLOWING*
G *OD'S INFINITELY*
S *UBLIME AND PERFECT PLAY TO UNFOLD IN OUR LIVES, LIKE A GENTLY*

O *PENING ROSEBUD WHOSE INTOXICATING*
F *RAGRANCE CAN ONLY BE EXPERIENCED*

W *HEN THAT "BEAUTY" IS FULLY*
A *WAKE, OR REVEALED,*
I *N ALL ITS NATURAL MAGNIFICENCE,*
T *AKES A CERTAIN*
I *NNER STRENGTH AND KNOWING THAT OUR WAITING IS*
N *OT EVER, EVER*
G *OING TO BE IN VAIN......HOW COULD IT BE?*

Love, Michael

11-08-2005

The non-rhyming poem on the previous page, "THE BLESSINGS OF WAITING", is the latest of 100's of pieces that I've written over the years, all of them with different titles and words, but all of them also with the same theme: Recognize God's Voice in your Heart and then follow it unconditionally as you start to AWAKEN and REMEMBER your TRUE IDENTITY as a CHILD OF GOD. During the first 5 years after my 40th birthday, I was privileged to have channelings not only with Diana and Beloved Master Merlin, but also with a lady named Virginia who channeled Beloved Master Jesus. Since you don't really know me, and even if you do, the term "channeling" might be a bit repulsive to you......and for good reason. There are many out there who claim to speak for this entity or that, and some of them are PURE channels whose personalities are totally out of the message......but they are rare. In the end, one's own "TRUTH CHECKER" must be the final judge in determining the veracity of the message. Although my own ego/personality still wants to pooh pooh Beloved Master Merlin's words, and even call Him names when despair creeps in, I HAVE ALWAYS KNOWN IN MY HEART that Beloved Master Merlin invariably spoke to me only with LOVE and WISDOM.

So, why have I shared this with you? Let's see. In December, 1987, I wrote a poem titled: "THE PEACE OF PATIENCE" where I speak of my desire to do more than I was currently doing in the world....... something more "Gandhi-esque", if you will. The last verse went:

BUT FIRST I KNOW THAT I MUST LEARN
TO TRUST IN GOD AND NOT TO YEARN,
TO HAVE FAITH THAT EACH EXPERIENCE
IS NEEDED AND HELPS ME GROW LESS "DENSE"

During my birthday channeling, Beloved Master Merlin shared: "........don't be so limited in your thinking to believe that your plan is better than God's plan.....God knows best....". In June, 1989, He shared: "......never question where you are, what you're doing or whom you're doing it with.....just BE THERE because you are there......". After all these years, as recently as last month, even though my Beloved

Elspeth and I have a LOVELY home which we call "THE CHRISTIE LIGHTHOUSE", despite the fact that she and I each received the same message from our Souls 4 years ago : "....live and work where you want, but please stay in the 4 corners area....", I still wanted to sell the house and start driving South into Mexico, Central America and even South America, just to break the monotony.

And then a ONE-derful thing happened. Rather than resist me, my Beloved said she'd call the real estate agent in the morning and put the house on the market. Even though we've been through so much together these past 15 years, it was the first time that I TRULY felt that she was WITH me, and I was filled with a GREAT LOVE for her. As I began to project where we might go, not a single place in the world came to mind.....not one. I suddenly became very PEACEFUL and was totally content to stay where we were and continue to.....WAIT (....this was TRULY a BLESSING for me...).

Wait for what you might ask. It's a good question with my only answer being: "......I don't know, but when it comes, I'll know it and I'll be ready to play my part....whatever that may be.....". For sure I'm waiting for the changes that will bring an end to a world of fear and separation and usher in the age of LOVE and UNITY, or, as the ancients referred to it: "THE GOLDEN AGE OF PEACE AND INNOCENCE". This last statement is both my and Elspeth's HEARTS' desire. It's been said that "patience" is the distance, in time, between an idea and its manifestation. In the book "SIDDARTHA" by Herman Hesse, Siddartha, who would later become THE BUDDHA, said that no matter what was happening in his life, ".....he could think, he could fast and he could wait...." and those three would allow him to handle any situation.

In my dictionary, the word "wait" is described: vb 1. to remain inactive in readiness or expectation. 2 to act as attendant or servant. 3 to be ready. My Beloved and I both work at WAL-MART as cashiers, each of us serving 100's of people every day. Lately, I've been sharing with some that I'm feeling a great expectancy, not like a child at Christmas, but more of a feeling that: SOMETHING ONE-DERFUL IS GOING TO HAPPEN. It's not just wishful thinking.....it's very, very REAL to me. The wars in Afghanistan and Iraq, the proliferation of nuclear weapons in India, Pakistan, North Korea and Iran, hurricane Katrina which flooded the city of New Orleans, hurricanes Rita, Wilma, Alpha and Beta which have marked an all time high for hurricanes in one season, the 7.6 magnitude earthquake in Pakistan which killed over 70,000 and left over 3 million homeless with winter fast approaching, all indicate to me that the world situation is beginning to unravel..... and that is a good...God thing. Whatever it takes to let the HEARTS of the world begin to TRULY open wide to both extend and receive GOD'S UNCONDITIONAL LOVE is a Blessing. If the events of the world, however harsh, help people to shift from an ego/personality centered consciousness, to a Soul/God centered consciousness where everything is ONE, then.....SO BE IT!

It's been said that: "......there are no atheists in foxholes.....". There are all sorts of "alarm" clocks out there to AWAKEN people when it's time to begin a NEW DAY; everything from the old fashioned clanging bell, to the gentle strains of a babbling brook and birds singing,....the choice is ours. It appears to me that time is rapidly running out on our choices of AWAKENING, and soon, as with the foxhole people, we'll only be left with the shrill, clanging bell. Just as a body part can be amputated by a butcher with a meat cleaver and you "biting a bullet", or by a skilled surgeon using a razor sharp scalpel as you gently sleep under anesthesia, while both methods achieve the same result, which would you choose?

Many, many years ago, I broke open a fortune cookie with the message: ".....We live in an eternity, the time to be HAPPY is NOW...". While I understood the words, I didn't fully grasp their meaning...... until last month, as I WAIT-ed on a customer. We were discussing how it seems that everyone in the world is suffering from a "GLOBAL EPIDEMIC OF HASTE".....we are like hamsters on a treadmill thinking that if we go faster, then we'll get there sooner. Outside of the obvious cardio-vascular benefits, what's the point? If we live in an

Eternity, then time does not REALLY, TRULY matter (....a MASTER never rushes, and we are all MASTERS who've forgotten that fact...). In discussing TIME, Einstein said : "......without TIME, everything would happen at once...". I never got a beginner's explanation of his "SPECIAL THEORY OF RELATIVITY".....energy = mass x the speed of light squared....but he understood that TIME IS RELATIVE. All that I've read over the past 19 years indicates that TIME is merely an ILLUSION. If you watch a parade from a place on the sidewalk, then you get a good idea of time.....from the first drum major, to the final float, you see the beginning, middle and end of the parade, during a period of TIME of, perhaps, 2 hours. Now, if you are in a helicopter, far above the parade, then you can see the entire show.....ALL AT ONCE.....just as Einstein pointed out......TIME does, indeed march on. TIME allows us to savor, or en-JOY, each moment. It also allows us to dread and curse each moment.....the choice is ours.

Wisdom says: ".....Time is gentle to those who always FOLLOW THEIR HEARTS.....". While I don't believe that there's an ULTIMATE URGENCY, this is, as the Hindu's call it : God's "lila", or sportive play, and it's time for each of us to play our part because......THE SHOW MUST GO ON! However, as Beloved Lord Buddha pointed out over 2,500 years ago: "......the pot of boiling water is unconcerned about the DESTINY of the bubble.....".

During His "Sermon on the Mount", Beloved Master Jesus gave us THE LORD'S PRAYER and THE BEATITUDES (which are reinterpreted by me in this book). When He said:

"...Blessed are the meek, for they shall inherit the Earth...", my interpretation of that Beatitude in the "BE-Attitudes" was: ".....Beings are those who always follow their Hearts, Because they KNOW they are doing GOD'S WILL.....".

My dictionary defines "meek" as: humbly PATIENT or docile (readily trained or taught), as under provocation from others. Since this work is about the BLESSINGS of PATIENCE and TRUST, and

FOLLOWING ONE's HEART, well, there you have that ONE-derful consistency of TRUTH. It's been said that "....where there is TRUTH, there can be no conflict....". Back in 1988, Beloved Master Merlin defined TRUE HUMBLENESS as: ".......the ability to allow all beings to see the LIGHT, the GOD, the PEACE, the LOVE, the TRUTH, the BEAUTY within your BEING......". To an ego/personality that is an impossible row to hoe but, when one identifies with their own SOUL, knowing Who they, and everyone else, are, then it's really quite easy.... and FUN....to BE DIVINELY HUMBLE (this last REVELATION may have just given me, being a cashier at WAL-MART, the answer to the question: "....are we having FUN yet?...").

Recently, my Beloved Elspeth and I explored a new job opportunity. She dug up her resumé and I typed a letter with my life's job history and we went to fill out applications. Even though our 7 year anniversary with WAL-MART, which would provide us with full vestment in the profit sharing program and 3 weeks vacation, was just a few months away, we were both willing to "go for it" and begin a new career..... at the "advanced" ages of 58 and 59. They never called us for an interview, but the exercise showed both of us that we were ready and eager to move beyond our "comfort zone" in a HEARTbeat. That fact is very exciting to both of us. We will continue to serve the people at WALLY WORLD and continue PURIFYING our personalities of their fear-based ("A COURSE IN MIRACLES" says: "....what is not LOVE, is simply fear....") ego effects until such time as we are called upon to do something else. As Tom Hanks' character in THE TERMINAL, Victor Navorski, said to the airport director who was trying to get Victor to leave the terminal illegally: "......I wait......". And so will we.

This essay evolved into something more than the "BLESSINGS OF WAITING", and that always excites me for I KNOW that WHO I AM is speaking to me and us via my body/personality (the "hide and seek" game continues). During the last encounter I was to have with Beloved Master Merlin, in November, 1991, He shared that as we continue to evolve, we would be 95% Soul and 5% personality. "A COURSE IN MIRACLES" refers to the body/personality as a "communication device".......simply a tool to be used by the Soul in this 3rd dimensional reality. As the astronauts needed their space suits to survive and communicate on the moon, so, too, do we Souls need our "time and space" suits to function and communicate in this world. Of course, let's keep in mind that as we EXPAND OUR MINDS, as Beloved Master Jesus did, the limitations of time and space just disappear.......like an early morning fog. But that's another story. My final word is simply.......ENJOY THE SHOW AND BE WHO YOU TRULY, REALLY ARE.

I feel that this round of writings, which began with THE LAMPLIGHTER in 1990, has come to an end. I have no idea if any future works will be created, but this particular theme, THE AWAKENING, has been completed so, in that LIGHT, I will say......... FINIS!

"MY AFFIRMATION OF TRUTH AND INNER PEACE"

THE LIGHT OF GOD SURROUNDS ME.....
....AND INFUSES ME

THE LOVE OF GOD ENFOLDS ME.....
....AND RADIATES FROM ME

THE POWER OF GOD PROTECTS ME.....
....AND ENLIVENS ME

THE PRESENCE OF GOD WATCHES OVER ME.....
....AND ALL OF CREATION

AND WHEREVER I AM, GOD IS.....
....AND SO BE IT!

Nineteen years ago today, on my 40th birthday, Diana, who was Beloved Master Merlin's "mouthpiece", began that first channeling with the above prayer/affirmation, minus the parts of each statement that are separated by dots. I was in-SPIRED to add those words many years later......to just expand what the statement means to me, and of course, ultimately, to all of us.

At the end of "THE BLESSINGS OF WAITING", I stated that I felt that the "LAMPLIGHTER" writings were completed, but I was pleasantly surprised to find this little gem under a pile of papers. GOD BLESS US........EVERYONE!!

Love, Michael

11-25-2005

"ALL TRUE PRAYERS ARE ANSWERED"

A *LL AT ONCE, IT CAME TO ME THAT*
L *IFE IS AS WE WANT IT TO BE. THE*
L *ESS TIME WE TAKE TO DISCOVER THIS TRUTH,*

T *HE SOONER WE GET TO ENJOY LIFE'S SWEET FRUITS. WE*
R *EALLY WERE MEANT TO LIVE LIKE GREAT KINGS,*
U *PON OUR DISCERNING THE UNITY IN*
E *VERYTHING. THE TRUE, HEARTFELT*

P *RAYERS OF GOD'S CHILDREN ON EARTH, ARE*
R *AYS OF INTENTION AIMED*
A *T PROVING THEIR WORTH. ASK AND*
Y *OU SHALL RECEIVE IS A STATEMENT OF TRUTH,*
E *VEN BETTER IS TO LET WISHING*
R *EMAIN BACK IN YOUR YOUTH. AS WE GROW AND*
S *EE THINGS WITH CRYSTAL CLARITY,*

A *LL NEEDS ARE PROVIDED WHEN WE SIMPLY JUST "BE"*
R *EMEMBRANCE OF OUR SOURCE IS AS*
E *ASY AS PIE,*

A *LL THAT'S REQUIRED IS TO SEE WITH GOD'S EYES*
N *O MORE DESIRES, OF COURSE YOU CAN*
S *TILL HAVE 'EM, BUT*
W *HY SETTLE FOR LESS THAN THE*
E *TERN' KINGDOM OF HEAVEN?*
R *IGHT HERE AND RIGHT NOW,*
E *VERY DAY OF YOUR LIFE, IS GOD'S*
D *IVINE ANSWER TO ALL OF YOUR STRIFE.*

Love, Michael
4-22-2006
"Earth Day" The 16th anniversary of my arrival in Lhasa, Tibet

When I completed "THE BLESSINGS OF WAITING" in November, 2005, I stated that I'd felt that the "LAMPLIGHTER" writings, which had been dealing with "THE AWAKENING" since their 1989 beginning, were concluded and that a new round of writings would emerge in the future. Alas, I must quote Peter Lorre's character in "CASABLANCA" who started to say something like ".....but I thought...." to Bogart's character, only to have Bogie snap back ".....you thought what..." to which Lorre replies : "......of course, what right have I to think?....". The poem on the previous page came to me a couple of weeks ago to my delightful surprise. So, let's see what my TRUE SELF wants to share with us today.

The poem that was created with the words "ALL TRUE PRAYERS ARE ANSWERED" was inspired by my viewing of the "extra features" on the "CAPOTE" DVD. The director and the cinematographer were explaining how everything seemed to miraculously fall into place during the filming of the picture. No matter how seemingly daunting the obstacle, the solution to the problem manifested at the right moment. It occurred to me that all sincere wishes, no matter how trivial, were always granted. As I write this, another proviso, in addition to sincerity, comes to mind. The wish must arise from a place of high intent with no desire to harm another. Certainly Hitler wanted to conquer and dominate the world with an iron fist, and for a time it looked like he might succeed. Because tens of millions suffered and died due to Nazi terror, the wish was tainted with FEAR, and therefore became an aberration that was eventually terminated.

I'm not suggesting that the FORCES OF LIFE "take sides" in worldly matters, but there are UNIVERSAL LAWS that we Souls on Earth live under, and those laws must be respected and honored. When I compiled my writings for a second version of "THE LAMPLIGHTER" in December, 1991, I'd just concluded my interpretation of "THE TEN COMMANDMENTS" which I titled: "10". As I'd done with "THE OUR FATHER" and "THE BEATITUDES" in version one, I juxtaposed the original words from the OLD TESTAMENT with my current understanding of what those teachings meant in the modern world.

Here is that particular "commandment":

"THE TEN COMMANDMENTS"	***"10"***
Thou shalt not kill	*Allow your brothers to Be Who they are NOW… And Revere all Life*

Whether OLD TESTAMENT or LAMPLIGHTER, we can see that Hitler wasn't playing by "the rules" and ultimately he reaped what he had sown. No condemnation or judgment, just a lesson to be experienced and, hopefully, learned…..at the Soul level. Interestingly, both Hitler and Gandhi were on the planet at the same time offering the world opposite ways to try to accomplish their goals…..Hitler via violence or "himsa", and Gandhi through non-violence or "ahimsa".

During one of his fasts, while being attended to by a female follower, Gandhi responded to the lady's comment that perhaps his fast was not "right", with the following: "…..When I despair, I remember that all through history, the way of TRUTH and LOVE has always won. There have been tyrants and murderers and, for a time, they can seem invincible, but, in the end, they always fall. Think of it….always…..". Of course Gandhi's dream of an independent India was spoiled by the religious division between the Hindu's and the Muslim's which led to the creation of two countries, India and Pakistan, and, ultimately, to Gandhi's assassination at the hands of a Hindu. His prayer or wish was granted, but in the end, as with Hitler, it didn't quite work out. So, what's the answer here?

It seems to me that most Souls come to Earth to experience the seemingly infinite variety of roles available to them. Hero and villain, victim and victimizer, cop and robber, rich man and poor man, saint and sinner, emperor and peasant, etc., etc., until the Soul decides that this was all very interesting and fun, but it's had enough of all the drama and just wants to "BE" WHO IT TRULY IS……Spirit encased in flesh and blood whose TRUE, DIVINE NATURE is that of a LOVING, GOD-CREATED BEING of ENERGY commonly known as a SOUL.

Rumi, the Sufi mystic who lived in the 13th century wrote: "….Beyond the field of good and evil there is a field……I'll meet you there…..". Shakespeare, who lived in the 16th century wrote: "…..Life is a tale told by an idiot, full of sound and fury, signifying……nothing..". "We dance round in a ring and suppose, But the Secret sits in the middle and knows," Robert Frost wrote. In the 4th century BC, a Wise entity wrote, "When we understand, we are at the center of the circle, and there we sit while Yes (good?) and No (evil?) chase each other around the circumference."

Did all these ONE-derful Souls just "get it" out of the blue? I believe that this Truth cannot be learned, it must be experienced and felt deeply in the Soul, as certainly as we "know" that 2+2=4. But even that example does not convey a True KNOWINGNESS, since arriving at 2+2=4 requires the application of certain assumptions or postulates (something that is assumed to be true). Rene Descartes wrote: "….I think, therefore, I AM….", but who is he? The body-personality known as Descartes? If that's the truth, then he is long since dead and buried. I AM……not!

Many years ago, someone advised: "…Let go of longing and aversion, and everything will be perfectly clear….". During this life's journey, I've had numerous "longings", as well as quite a few "aversions". Most of the longings were material in nature, such as getting a black Pontiac Trans Am, working in the General Office of GTE of California, making a pilgrimage to Tibet, vacationing in Tahiti, finding my Golden Girl or Soul Mate, etc., etc. All of those granted wishes did not get me any closer to my own Soul, or the LORD GOD OF MY BEING. With those ONE-derful Souls in Tibet and with my Beloved Elspeth, the GOD within them was and is quite visible. There are no more longings except for wanting to "REMEMBER" WHO I TRULY AM. I know I must let go of that one and just let it happen.

As far as aversions go, I've quite a number of those as well: speaking before an audience, extending LOVE to rude people, having to go to a job every day, being around self righteous, holier than thou people, wow, there's a whole bunch that I've been working on for 20 years and yet I'm still holding on to them.

All these years of writing have proven to me that I AM THE SOUL, these ONE-derful words could not possibly come from my brain.....they're too PURE, WISE and LOVING. As of this day, I will be very aware of every longing and aversion, and I'll send it on its way, thanking it for its contribution to my AWAKENING. My prayer is simply this.......NO MORE PRAYERS.....JUST BE WHO I AM.

My Beloved Friend and Mentor, Beloved Master Merlin/aka Sanat Kumara, once advised me: "......Seek no thing; just BE where you are because you are there, and stay in the present moment....".

During a channeling that my Beloved Elspeth had with Master Merlin, I was invited to sit in for the last portion of it. As I entered the room, Beloved Master Merlin said: ".....ahh, enter the hero......what is the hero, Michael?....". I responded that the hero is the one who saves the day. Upon hearing my response, Beloved Master Merlin asked me: "......How does that (role) keep you separated from God?....". After having written the previous pages, I TRULY understand His question.....I and my Creator are ONE. As Paramahansa Yogananda once said: "....We are all Soul waves on the Sea of GOD's SPIRIT...".

So, to summarize this essay and extract its essence: Yes, all prayers, whether of LIGHT or darkness, are answered".....be sure of what you ask for, because you most likely will receive it.....", is a gentle warning to beware of God's sense of humor. Since the 23rd Psalm assures us that "....the Lord is our Shepherd, we shall (can) not want....", and since it's been said that God knows what we need before we do, we will always have what we need. When we stop asking for "stuff" and just content ourselves with "BEING" Happy to go with the flow, KNOWING that as GOD-created Souls we will always be looked after, enjoy your LIFE, remove the idea of separation from your mind, and just BE your unique ex-PRESSION of GOD.....and THE CREATOR will be well pleased....SO BE IT.....AUM...and...AMEN!

"BE TRUE TO YOUR NATURE"

B *EFORE WE CAME HERE, WE WERE OH, SO PURE,*
E *ACH SOUL WAS PREPARED FOR THE TESTS 'TWOULD ENDURE,*

T *HE GIFTS WE WERE GIVEN AT THE TIME OF CREATION,*
R *EFLECTED OUR FATHER , WITHOUT HESITATION*
U *SING THESE GIFTS OF LOVE, JOY AND PEACE, WOULD*
E *NABLE US TO SHARE THEM WITH ALL WHOM WE'D MEET*

T *HE PLAN WAS A GOOD ONE, IT MADE PERFECT SENSE, BUT*
O *NCE WE ARRIVED HERE, WE BECAME VERY DENSE*

Y *OUNG PEOPLE WERE TAUGHT ALL SORTS OF REPRESSION,*
O *UR TRUE NATURES WERE BLOCKED, FROM THEIR FULL EXPRESSION*
U *NLIKE GOD'S LOWER CREATURES, WHO CAN ONLY BE TRUE, THE*
R *EASON WE CAME HERE GOT HIDDEN FROM VIEW. IT'S*

N *EVER TOO LATE TO MAKE A CORRECTION,*
A *ND REMIND EVERYONE OF THEIR IMMINENT ASCENSION. JUST*
T *AKE THE TIME, AND TUNE IN TO YOUR HEART, AND*
U *SE WHAT GOD GAVE YOU RIGHT FROM THE START*
R *EMEMBER YOUR SOURCE, WITH ALL OF YOUR MIGHT, AND*
E *ARTH WILL BECOME THAT BRIGHT BEACON OF LIGHT*

Love, Michael

11-25-2006
(The 20th anniversary of my 40th Birthday)

Well, am I surprised! After deciding on October 1st, 2006 to compile my 20 years' worth of writings into a manuscript for publication, I thought there wouldn't be anything else new to be included.......I keep stumbling over the Peter Lorre lesson (...what right have I to think?...). As I was lounging in bed one morning last month, through the skylight in our bedroom, I observed a flock of geese passing overhead. I was reminded of the documentary "WINGED MIGRATION" which, through incredible photography, tracked the annual, circuitous, and sometimes tortuous, routes of various species of birds......some of whom traveled many thousands of miles to get to their destination. They gave no thought to weather, safety, food, shelter or any other "human" concern...they did it because that was the way they were Created. They were simply being True to their natures. The words "BE TRUE TO YOUR NATURE" came to me and...here we are again.

Being True to one's nature reminded me of a story. In ancient India, while a man was relaxing on the banks of the Ganges River, he noticed a scorpion floundering in the water, being overpowered by the current. Just as it was disappearing beneath the waves, a passerby appeared and lifted the scorpion to safety on the bank. After the creature regained its composure, it proceeded to sting the man who just saved its life. The observer noted that the good Samaritan was a member of the Brahmin, or highest, caste of the Hindu society (Brahmin translates as "knower of God"). A little later, the man saw the scorpion in the water again, only to be rescued by the Brahmin who was subsequently stung. After 3 acts of this drama, the man approached the Brahmin and asked him why he kept saving the scorpion only to be repeatedly stung. The Brahmin replied: "...My brother, the scorpion was just being a scorpion, and I, because I am a Brahmin, was just being a Brahmin....".

Another story I enjoy has to do with the movie "THE GREAT SANTINI", in which Robert Duvall plays the title character, a macho, no nonsense Marine pilot who lives his life and rules his family as if they were recruits and he were the drill instructor. "The Great Santini" is just a nickname for the character's real name which is "Bull" Mitchum. Towards the end of the movie, "Bull" is on a routine flight when his plane develops engine trouble and, rather than eject and have the plane crash in a residential neighborhood, he flies out to sea where he is killed in the crash. Before the mother and teenage children depart for the funeral, she admonishes the children to "....shed your tears now, because no child of Bull Mitchum is going to be seen crying in public....". It struck that me if children of a human parent stifled their grief to honor their earthly father, why couldn't Children of a Divine Parent make the effort to honor their Heavenly Parent by Being the Children of God that they Truly were?

Here are some quotes from the New Testament which encourage us to ex-press our Divinity, as Beloved Master Jesus did:

> *"...Do not be overcome by evil, but overcome evil with good..."*
>
> *Romans 12:21*

> *"...Resist not evil (with evil). But whoever slaps you on your right cheek, turn the other to him also..."*
>
> *Matthew 5:39*

These verses were saying the same thing: Evil should be "resisted" only with its logically effective opposite.....Good or Love. Friedrich Nietzsche (1844-1900) once said: "...The unchangeable character can be influenced in its <u>expression</u> by education and environment, but not in its essence....". If you were walking alongside your worst enemy, and he or she happened to trip and fall down, what would your first reaction be? Would it would go against your True Nature to not help them up?

Humankind has been spurring itself on to all sorts of un-God-like behavior since time immemorial. During the past 150 years, we've had "...Remember the Alamo...", "...Remember the Maine...", "...Remember Pearl Harbor...", and most recently:
"...Remember 9-11...". As AWAKENING Children of God, these war rallies do not serve us anymore. "...Flight or fight..." was OK for our ancestors, but now we must adopt a "..Stay and discuss.." philosophy, with the same intention: CONTINUATION.

Many years ago, I read a work by a Soul named Baird T. Spalding titled: "LIFE and TEACHING of the MASTERS of the FAR EAST" in which he details his 1894 visit, along with 10 other scientists, to India and Tibet, and what transpired during the 3 ½ years that they lived and worked with the Great Masters of the Himalayas. There were so many beautiful words and ideas expressed in the books, and a few of them are always in the forefront of my consciousness:

> *"...The trees of society that have not been planted in Truth, shall eventually be uprooted..."*
>
> *"...AMERICA is an anagram for: I AM RACE..."*

What did those Souls see in our future? Will the United States become a God Centered country which will be a True Beacon of Light for the rest of the world and our neighbors in the Cosmos? It's been said that the Mayan calendar ends in 2012, signifying the "end of the world". Does that mean the end of all the un-God-like behavior and the beginning of a "...One for All and All for One..." consciousness? Can you imagine how quickly the world would change if "...survival of the fittest..." were replaced with "...thrival (I just coined a new word) for everyone..."?

Earlier in "SNIPPETS FROM MY SOUL", I shared that there were no 2 grains of sand alike. So, if a simple thing like sand can have so many different expressions, I guess that all the different expressions in this book on the theme of "...Being True to One's True and Radiant Self...", are just the tip of the Cosmic Iceberg. Thank you for purchasing and reading my opus. If the Truth within you was touched in any way, then I have served you and our Creator in some measure and for that, I AM most GRATEFUL!

GOD BLESS US EVERYONE!

Author's note: Back on 8-01-1998, my Beloved Elspeth wrote a poem titled: "A CHILD OF GOD" , and since it talks about a lot of what this work discusses, I'd like to share it with you. I hope you enjoy it.

"A CHILD OF GOD"

by Ellie 8-01-1998
Vermont

We're born into this world innocent and clear
Knowing only to LOVE without any fear
Perhaps cuddled and nurtured by parents dear
Whose voices sound soothing to our ear

We slumber in gentle peaceful bliss
Our foreheads brushed tenderly with a kiss
Life should always be like this
Snuggled and cozy in a bundled abyss

Not one single care, no need to worry
Nowhere to go, no plan to hurry
No thought of our safety or for making money
We just coo and ga ga and make faces so funny!

As days go by we live and learn
The once nurturing looks grow hard and stern
There are "do's" and "don'ts" at every turn
Our softness and tenderness lost in the churn

Half truths are instilled...years go by
And soon we begin to believe in the lie
That we are not good enough so we wait "to die"
Simply "going with the flow" we forget to try

Heart doors grow creaky and dark with rust
In the haze of all our Earthly musts
We forget our beginnings...forget to trust
In the purity and sweetness that is DIVINELY us!

I believe our TRUE nature is just to be free
Full of wonder and childlike simplicity
Knowing OUR Father will meet any need
Embracing all on Earth with each LOVING deed

AFTERWORD

Christmas is only 2 short days away, and I guess it's fitting that I write this last little snippet as a means of closing out the past 20 years of my Life. Many years ago, Beloved Master Merlin shared that, rather than there being just a single Example of Divine Love Which Beloved Master Jesus ex-Pressed, at this point in time, Mother Earth was preparing to give birth to 1000's of Christs. Since I believe that each of us is a cell in the body of Christ, Merlin's words sounded True to me.

The ministry of Beloved Master Jesus affected 1000's during the time He walked the planet 2,000 years ago, and billions more since then. It's fun and exciting to IMAGINE the impact 5 or 10 thousand Christs, spread all across the globe, would have on the people and our Beloved Mother Earth. As Beloved Master Jesus said:

"....And I, if I be lifted up, draw all Souls up with Me....."

Perhaps, in 2007, we'll start Creating Heaven...

God Bless us......Everyone!

Love, your Soul Brother, Michael
Christmas, 2006

ABOUT THE AUTHOR

Michael A Christie was born in Brooklyn, New York , in 1946, and attended Brooklyn Preparatory High School and Brooklyn College. This is his first published work. He currently lives in the 4 Corners area, in Bayfield Colorado, with his Beloved Twin Flame, Elspeth. You can reach him at PO Box 1734, Bayfield, Co. 81122

www.ingramcontent.com/pod-product-compliance
Ingram Content Group UK Ltd.
Pitfield, Milton Keynes, MK11 3LW, UK
UKHW041848190726
13854UKWH00002B/772

9 781425 109035